Golden and Blue Like My Heart

Golden and Blue Like My Heart

Masculinity, Youth, and Power Among Soccer Fans in Mexico City

Roger Magazine

The University of Arizona Press   Tucson

The University of Arizona Press
© 2007 The Arizona Board of Regents
All rights reserved

Library of Congress Cataloging-in-Publication Data
Magazine, Roger, 1969–
Golden and blue like my heart : masculinity, youth, and power
among soccer fans in Mexico City / Roger Magazine.
p. cm.
Includes bibliographical references and index.
ISBN 978-0-8165-2637-6 (hardcover : alk. paper)
ISBN 978-0-8165-2693-2 (pbk.: alk. paper)
1. Soccer—Social aspects—Mexico. 2. Soccer fans—Mexico—
Attitudes. 3. Youth—Mexico—Political activity. 4. Masculinity—
Mexico. 5. Democracy—Mexico. 6. Pumas (Soccer team). I. Title.
GV943.9.S64M34 2007
796.33409725'3—dc22   2007003685

Manufactured in the United States of America on
acid-free, archival-quality paper.

12 11 10 09   6 5 4 3 2

To the memory of
Eduardo Archetti, friend and teacher,
and of Ricardo Abud, El Zague

Contents

Figures

Acknowledgments

The research on which this book is based was made possible by a dissertation grant from the Wenner-Gren Foundation for Anthropological Research. A Fulbright Scholarship provided a year of funding for writing my dissertation in the Department of Anthropology at the University of Oslo, Norway, and generous support for additional research was provided by the Universidad Iberoamericana's Dirección de Investigación.

Far too many people have participated in or supported me in this project over the past ten years to mention them all. Numerous people at the University of Arizona Press contributed to the completion of this book. In particular, I would like to thank Allyson Carter for her interest in the project, two anonymous readers for their suggestions, and Lisa DiDonato for her precise and thoughtful editing. I would also like to thank José Pedro Álvarez R. for granting permission to use his superb photographs of La Rebel.

I thank the graduate students in my urban anthropology seminars at the Universidad Iberoamericana over the past six years, who patiently listened to my ideas before providing useful criticism. I am grateful to Elaine Carey, Richard Giulianotti, and David Wood for encouraging me to publish my research as a book and to Carmen Bueno for her constant support. I am indebted to Chris McIntyre and Casey Walsh for tolerantly listening to me work out my ideas. I sincerely thank Elizabeth Ferry and Sarah Hill for reading and commenting on earlier versions of the manuscript and for our stimulating exchanges of ideas over the years. I am also indebted to Sidney Mintz and Patricia Fernández-Kelly for their suggestions and advice during the formulation of the project. My advisors, Michel-Rolph Trouillot and Gillian Feeley-Harnik, provided invaluable guidance as I was writing my dissertation.

During the 1998–1999 academic year the Department of Anthropology at the University of Oslo generously provided a workspace and hospitality. Among them, I am particularly indebted to Christian Krohn-Hansen and Marit Melhuus for taking the time to read and comment on my work. Above all, I would like to acknowledge the contributions of my friend and teacher, the late Eduardo Archetti, whose passion for life and anthropology continues to provide me with inspiration. He whole-heartedly supported me and this project; even more importantly, he taught me to believe in my work and to approach it with passion.

This study would not have been possible if the members of the Porra Plus had not received me into their fold in 1996. I express my gratitude not only for their acceptance but also for teaching me what it means to be a Puma. More specifically, I thank Charlie, David (Don Ramón), Edgar, Fernando (Ponchito), Fernando (El Poli), Guillermo (Fito), Miguel Ángel, and Victor for their assistance and their friendship. I am especially indebted to Sergio for his appreciation of what I was trying to do and for patiently guiding me toward an understanding of Pumas' fandom. My greatest debt from the field is to the late Ricardo Abud (El Zague), who introduced me to the Plus, shared with me his wisdom, and honored me with his friendship.

I express my gratitude to my parents, Joan Magazine and Michael Magazine, for their unconditional encouragement and support. My son, Matthew, like a good Puma, reminds me daily that there is more to life than work. My wife, Cristina Cedillo Ruiz, not only provides a critical intellectual eye from outside the discipline but is always there to offer support when I falter.

A List of Informants

Because it may be difficult for readers to remember the numerous informants referred to in the text, I have provided this list as a reference. Please note that I have changed all my informants' names as well as some biographic details to protect their anonymity. I refer here to the informants' ages in 1996.

El Caco. A twenty-two-year-old porra member from a working-class neighborhood near the center of Mexico City. His reputation as a fearless street-tough (he is rumored to be a thief and drug dealer) gives him minor celebrity status among other porra members. At moments, however, his class distance from other members provokes some teasing, related, for example, to his pronunciation of certain words in a typical inner-city, popular manner.

César. A nineteen-year-old porra member with aspirations to study at the National Autonomous University of Mexico (UNAM), but who recently left high school just before finishing to get a job and help support his mother and younger brother, with whom he lives in the eastern part of the city.

Daniel. A twenty-five-year-old office clerk who is currently earning a bachelor's degree at a private university, using his wages to pay the tuition. He lives with his parents in the eastern part of the city.

Ernesto. The porra's president and a graduate of the UNAM. He is about fifty years old and works as a lawyer at a government agency. His wife and two teenage children occasionally attend games and sit with the porra. The porra members frequently refer to him as "Licenciado," a term commonly used to refer to lawyers, or "Lic" for short.

Gerardo. A twenty-one-year-old porra member who studies engineering at the UNAM and lives with his parents in the southern part of the city. He is one of the founding members of the subsection of the porra known as La Rebel Plus. His charisma makes him one of a few informal leaders among his peers and thus also a target of the president's efforts to create loyal clients.

Héctor. A twenty-five-year-old accountant who lives with his parents on the southern edge of the city.

Javier. The porra's founder and president up until he left the group in 1995, when Ernesto took over as president. A charismatic man in his late thirties, he ruled the porra as a sort of benevolent dictator.

Jorge. A twenty-two-year-old member who, like El Caco, was somewhat exceptional among porra members for his social background. He left home at the age of fifteen and joined a gang of street children. He lives in cheap hotels near the city center and makes money washing windshields and doing odd jobs.

José Luis. An eighteen-year-old porra member who studies at one of the UNAM's high schools and hopes to earn a university degree in computer science. He lives with his parents in the eastern part of the city.

Juan. A twenty-year-old fan who works for the city's subway system and hopes to study at the UNAM. With his charisma and loud booming voice, Ernesto chose him to succeed Rodolfo to lead the group's cheers. This choice was part of an effort to co-opt his position as informal leader among his peers.

Rafael. A twenty-one-year-old political science student at the UNAM who lives with his parents in the southern part of the city. Along with Gerardo, he is a founding member of La Rebel Plus.

Ramón. A twenty-two-year-old porra member who studies biology at the UNAM. Although not a member of La Rebel Plus, Ramón gets along well with its members and took a leading role in efforts to oust Ernesto from his position as president.

Rodolfo. In his late twenties, Rodolfo holds an engineering degree from the UNAM and works as a technician in a publishing business. He is a personal friend of Ernesto and led the cheers from el poste before Ernesto replaced him with Juan, in a effort to quell discontent among the younger members.

Rubén. A twenty-one-year-old porra member and a close friend of Juan.

Samuel. In his early sixties, Samuel is one of only a couple of porra members older than Ernesto. Unlike the younger members, he sees his support of the Pumas as inseparable from his duty as a graduate of the UNAM to uphold the values of honor, *educación* (good manners), and order that he associates with the university.

Golden and Blue Like My Heart

1

Introduction

Soccer Fandom and Competing Social Projects in Contemporary Mexico

It was late one Sunday afternoon in April 1996, and I had just returned from an away game against Pachuca with the other members of *una porra* (a cheering club) I had started attending Pumas games with just a couple of months before. The Pumas had been playing badly over the previous few weeks, but on that day they had played well and tied 1–1. Jorge invited me back to his house to watch more soccer and some American football on television. Surfacing at the Revolución metro station, we stopped at a stand for some tacos, and Jorge asked me what I had liked most about the game. I described the play in which the Pumas had scored the tying goal as well as the good performances of a couple of individual players. When I finished, it was clear that Jorge had his answer prepared. He said that what was truly special about the game for him was that *la porra de verdad apoyó al equipo* (the cheering club truly supported the team) and made a difference in the outcome of the game. He recalled that even though the Pumas was the away team, the club's cheering had drowned out the cheering of Pachuca's acclaimed porra, La Barra Tusa. Jorge said that he thought the team recognized this and appreciated it because the players came over after the game and gave us a Goya[1] (the team cheer). He noted that the Pumas' vice-president had even turned to the section where the porra was sitting and applauded us from his booth.

Only when I was writing up my field notes did I realized that from the beginning Jorge had asked the question to teach me

Figure 1. A Porra Plus member leading cheers.

something about being a Pumas fan and a porra member. He was trying to get across that their active support of the team distinguishes Pumas fans, and in particular the porra members, from other fans in Mexico. More specifically, porra members describe their own cheering as active and thus with the potential to produce inspired play, goals, and victories, whereas opposing fans cheer in a reactive or passive manner. They explain that opposing fans cheer only after their team scores a goal and that, even then, this cheering is a performance of the inauthentic loyalty of the client rather than a true heartfelt celebration.

This was just one of many lessons I received from porra members during my first months of fieldwork. Through these lessons, I came to understand that being a Pumas fan involves the construction and expression of a complex identity and ideal vision for society that intertwine notions of freedom, politics, youthfulness, and masculinity. In this book, I attempt to convey this complex identity and vision for the future and to document the members' struggles against competing visions of urban Mexico.

Over the last two decades, economic crises and their neoliberal remedies have loosened corporatist clientelism's hold on political culture in urban Mexico. This loosening has undoubtedly permitted the development of practices associated with democracy and the free market, most clearly exemplified by the signing of the North American Free Trade Agreement (NAFTA) in 1992 and by the defeat of the Partido Revolucionario Institucional (PRI) in the presidential elections in 2000 after holding the office for more than eighty years. As I have argued elsewhere (Magazine 2004b), in recent years authors have imagined Mexican political culture in dualistic terms, either as a tension between clientelism and liberal democracy or as a transition from the former to the latter. If an alternative beyond this clientelism-democracy dichotomy is considered at all, it is usually a worried cry of disorder and identity crisis, referring to those, usually imagined as young urban men, who have been cut loose from their clientelistic moorings without yet having been transformed into modern democratic citizens.

My research, however, has led me to believe that an incomplete transition to free-market democracy and neoliberalism's characteristic hands-off approach have made political culture into a contested space, where actors struggle to implement different social projects. In other words, neoliberalism has created a partial social vacuum allowing latent ideal visions and social projects to come to the fore, where they confront the remains of clientelism, an emerging individualistic democracy, and each other. Soccer, with its competitive nature and its inherent tensions between the individual and the collective and between freedom and control, has become a key site for actors to congregate and to imagine, contest, and implement these social alternatives in urban Mexico. While my focus here is on just one of these social alternatives and on just one team's fans, these would be difficult to understand without a discussion of Mexican soccer fandom more generally.

Team Choice and Identity in Contemporary Mexico

Sports fans in the United States are accustomed to fan loyalties based on territorial associations: one generally cheers for the team from the city where one was born or lives. The extensiveness of this territorial basis for fans' loyalties is fairly unique to the United States and Canada and is due, I think, to the relative urban decentralization of these countries. In many European and Latin American nations, where one city houses a large percentage of the country's urban population and an even larger portion of its economic and political power, the basis for many fans' loyalties goes beyond territorial associations. Because a number of professional teams—usually soccer teams—are based in these capital cities, residents must look to other criteria to choose their team. Often these criteria consist of class or ethnic associations, which may emerge from the characteristics of the neighborhood where the team plays or initially played its home games. Because most neighborhoods do not have their own teams, the teams come to represent the original neighborhood's class or ethnic characteristics for a wider following rather than just the neighborhood itself. Thus, supporting a particular team acts as a "socio-cultural marker" and says "much about the way supporters [see] themselves" (Edelman 2002:1443). Furthermore, this decentralized urban pattern influences fan loyalties in outlying cities as well. Because of these urban centers' disproportionate economic power, their teams can often buy the best players, which produces a dual effect, attracting some fans from outlying cities while provoking others' hatred. Furthermore, due to these cities' disproportionate cultural influence over the rest of the country, the class, ethnic, or other associations of its teams become well known in outlying cities, attracting still other fans. Even those fans in outlying cities who choose to follow their local team are influenced by the centralized urban pattern, in that rivalries tend to develop not between neighboring cities but between each outlying city and the teams from the capital.

Soccer fandom in Mexico is exemplary of this pattern, which is not surprising considering the extreme centralization of the country's economic and political power in its capital, Mexico City. While the Mexican professional soccer league consists of a total of twenty clubs, four of them—El América, Las Chivas, Cruz Azul, and Los Pumas—are known as "national teams" because they attract a nationwide rather than a regional following. Undoubtedly, many fans are drawn to one of these four teams because of their histories of success in the league. Of course, such success breeds more success because larger followings mean more income for the clubs, which in turn can be used to buy better players. However, all four teams are also associated with a set of values, from which it is basically impossible for a fan to separate his or her choice of team, because most Mexico City residents, including people with no interest in soccer itself, are familiar with these associations. Some fans may explicitly draw on these sets of values when talking about their fandom, while others simply state that they like the way their team plays. But even for the latter the association with a particular set is inescapable, and thus it almost surely has been taken into account in claiming one of the national teams as a favorite. In this sense, support of one of the national teams constitutes a public social action, a sociocultural marker, or an identity.

In my casual conversations with fans of all four teams, there emerged standard statements explaining team choice. América fans emphasize the fact that the club *tiene los mejores juga-dores* (has the best players). Fans of Las Chivas note that the team follows a creed of *puros mexicanos* (only Mexicans), refer-ring to the fact that it fields only Mexican players. Cruz Azul supporters often make some sort of reference to an association with the working class. Finally, Pumas fans mention the team's *filosofía de puros jóvenes* (philosophy of only youths). Fans and even nonfans make the same statements explaining other teams' attractions. In other words, there is general agreement over what each team represents among Mexico City residents, with the possible exception of América, as I will discuss further below.

These statements mean little to someone unfamiliar with life in urban Mexico. The fact that a team "has the best play-ers," for example, probably sounds like a statement that any fan might make about his favorite team. In fact, making such an apparently neutral statement among Mexico City residents evokes broader associations with a set of values and even "an ideal vision for Mexican society," as I call it (see below). These associations go well beyond soccer fandom, even if they are per-haps most clearly represented through support of one of the national teams. Because these broader associations are shared, Mexico City residents do not need to voice them, which made accessing them somewhat difficult for a new arrival like myself at the beginning of my fieldwork. Certain informants did elabo-rate upon these broader associations, but much of the under-standing that I gained is the product of my general familiarity with life in Mexico City—the holistic knowledge that anthropol-ogists insist is so important for understanding specific aspects of social life.

It is common knowledge in Mexico City that América is owned by the powerful television conglomerate Televisa. Also, there is a widespread close association between Televisa and the national and international elite because of the media company's consistently uncritical stance toward those in power (Magazine 2001), meaning mainly the PRI before its electoral defeat in 2000 and now a more diffuse agglomeration of the agents of international capitalism. Thus, for América fans and non-América fans alike, supporting the team means aligning oneself with those in power, including Televisa itself. Currently, this alignment involves displaying a combination of a commitment to new and old routes to power: neoliberalism and international capitalism versus *relaciones* (literally relations; patron-client relations). América itself displays these commitments, paying high salaries to international and national star players and then integrating them into the Televisa "family" from which all criticism, even when merited professionally, is absent.

The statement that América "has the best players" needs to be interpreted in this context: fans are expressing their desire to connect themselves to those who are closest to the top. When people refer to América as *el equipo de los ricos* (the team of the rich), they are referring to the club's direct link to the rich and powerful and not to the fans themselves, who come from all social strata, but especially from the *clases populares* (working class). Because of América's association with power, fans of the other three national teams consider it to be their biggest rival. While América fans and fans of the other teams all describe América in basically similar terms, the latter do so in a critical manner, often criticizing not only the team but those in power as well. In contrast, when opposing fans talk about the other three national teams and the values associated with them, they usually do so with indifference or even sometimes with respect. This widespread loathing of América is evidenced by the feminizing school-yard taunt, *Le vas al América y te sientas para mear* (You support América and you piss sitting down), which also exemplifies the extent to which the identities associated with the national teams organize social relations in urban Mexico well beyond the stadium.

The ideal vision for Mexican society associated with Las Chivas derives from the club's creed of puros mexicanos. The practice of refusing to import players matches a vision for Mexican society that constituted the dominant state strategy from the 1930s to the 1970s. Spurred by the anti-imperialist sentiments of the Mexican Revolution, the government appropriated and nationalized several major foreign-owned industries and created laws limiting imports and encouraging their substitution with Mexican products. Las Chivas are a holdout from this period, exemplifying an ideal of national autonomy by still using only Mexican "products." The fact that it is the only one of the four national teams located outside of Mexico City, in Guadalajara, the nation's second largest city, reinforces this association between the club and an autonomous nationalism. Guadalajara is the political and economic center of the region from which many of Mexico's national symbols have come, such as tequila and mariachis.[2]

The broader implications of supporting Cruz Azul arise from the fact that the club is owned by the cement cooperative of the same name. Because the company is owned and run by the workers and because cement is a material that so many working-class men handle in the construction industry and with which they aspire to build their houses,[3] the team is linked to a working-class identity and values. Its nickname, appropriately, is *la máquina azul* (the blue machine).

Like the Chivas' pure Mexicans ideal, the working-class vision represented by Cruz Azul enjoyed strong state support in the recent past. In the decades following the revolution, the government attempted to draw as many groups as possible into a single political body in an effort to maintain power and political stability. This strategy, commonly known as "state corporatism" and that I prefer to call "corporatist clientelism," functioned through the government's distribution of profits from nationalized industries (oil in particular) and import duties in exchange for loyalty from

labor unions and other organizations in the form of membership in a single political party. Cooperatives flourished with this
government support, but most have weakened or disappeared
entirely since the switch to neoliberal policy and the thinning of
state corporatism begun in the early 1980s.[4]

Thus, in the rivalries between América and these other two
teams, we can read the tensions resulting from recent and dra-
matic shifts in national political economic strategy. Supporting
Las Chivas or Cruz Azul is at least partly a call for a return to better
times and the Mexico of the recent past, when patron-client relations bore significant fruit even for those far from the top. Being
an América fan simultaneously represents support for global capitalism in Mexico and a willingness to enter loyally into patron-client relations even if the security provided formerly by corporatist
clientelism is now lacking.

The ideal vision for society associated with the fourth national
team, the Pumas of the National Autonomous University of Mexico, stems from its philosophy of puros jóvenes, which refers to the
fact that it fields only young players. This book is about a group of
Pumas fans, their version of the ideal vision that the team represents, and the practices and events through which they formulate,
struggle for, express, and sometimes contradict this vision. Briefly,
the ideal vision for society represented by the Pumas begins with
the philosophy of "only youths," but is not simply a question of
age. Most Pumas fans self-identify as youths and explain that they
are attracted to the team because of the perspective on life and
soccer that they share with the players. According to these fans,
the importance of being youths is that because they and the players have not yet been influenced by corruption and clientelism
or dulled by scientific objectivity or democratic rationality, they
are closer to something inherently and basically human: emotion. Without these negative influences that come to transform
and dominate older people after they have spent time in the world
of work and politics, they are free to experience genuine emotion
such as love, passion, or joy. Thus, their practices on the field, in
the stands, or in life in general are guided by something internal,

by emotions and not by dependence on others, as in clientelism, nor by external objective rules or logic as in democracy or the free market.

If América fans look to the best money can buy (whether Mexican or foreign) for their vision of soccer and society, Chivas fans to what is most Mexican, and Cruz Azul fans to the working class, then the Pumas fans look to the emotional capacity they see as inherently human. While Pumas fans see América and what it represents as their greatest rival, they do so in a way that also opposes them to the Chivas and Cruz Azul, which both represent a style of being Mexican closely associated with dependence on others in the form of corporatist clientelism. The Pumas' ideal vision shares with those of Chivas and Cruz Azul a critique of the present, but the return it proposes is not to the recent past but to something inherently human that is in danger of being obscured by any form of social structure or any political project.

Soccer and Soccer Fans in the Social Sciences

Studies of soccer and soccer fans have primarily focused on two world regions: Western Europe, especially England, and the southern cone of South America, principally Argentina and Brazil. Many of the studies of soccer fans in England were spurred by violence in and around stadiums instigated by so-called hooligans. These works try to explain fans' violent behavior and often suggest how it might be quelled. The most prominent of these were authored or coauthored by sociologist Eric Dunning (e.g., Elias and Dunning 1986; Dunning et al. 1987). Applying Norbert Elias's theory of the civilizing process, Dunning and others contended that hooligans come from the population segment on the tail end of the civilizing process and thus they are relics from a past when such violence was normal occurrence.[5] Such studies have in turn produced their share of critiques, often by researchers who themselves actively supported or support teams. Armstrong (1998), for example, argued that the hooligan studies do more to create the hooligan and define him as a social problem than provide understandings of fans' practices. He posited that these studies contain few data based on actual research among supporters and are based instead on preconceived assumptions and reports by police and the media. Because these studies are then used to justify sensationalist media reports and violent, disciplining police action, a conveniently closed circle is formed in which academics, the media, and state actors can rely on each other to support their endeavors without any interference from the facts surrounding actual fans.

In chapter 4, I follow Armstrong's lead and examine how the meanings of fans' practices derive from interactions between fans and state actors—in this case, primarily intellectuals writing about the "typical" urban Mexican man. However, my main interest in Armstrong's critique is his call for an ethnographic approach that seeks fans' own understandings of their actions. Several other authors, primarily focusing on European fans, have contributed to this effort (see Redhead, ed. 1993; Giulianotti et al., eds. 1994; Armstrong and Giulianotti, ed. 1997, 2001; Robson 2000; Edelman 2002), often showing how team choice can express complex identities, while resisting the outside observer's quick identification of meaningless violence, crowds, and hooligans. Bromberger et al. (1993:120), for example, suggested:

> If the supporters identify so intensely with their city's, their factory's or their national team, it is because this team is perceived, through its playing style as a symbol of a specific mode of collective existence, and not as a simple sign (arbitrary) of a common belonging. The 'style' of the team does not always correspond to the real practise of the players—who change year after year, obeying different tactics depending on the manager, fashion, etc.—but to a stereotyped image, rooted in tradition, that the collectivity gives to itself and wishes to give to others. Thus style is part of a 'mentalité' or a 'collective imaginary' in the sense used by M. Vovelle, not so much the way in which men live, but the manner in which it pleases them to recount their way of life.

To win is, without doubt, to affirm one's superiority, but it is also to experience the joy of imposing your own style, your own mark to the detriment of the others.

This idea of teams and playing styles as symbols of whole ways of life is comparable to Geertz's notion of the Balinese cockfight as "a Balinese reading of Balinese experience, a story they tell themselves about themselves" (Geertz 1973:448). What Bromberger et al., as well as the organization of professional soccer into multiple-team leagues, add to Geertz's formulation is the possibility of multiple visions and confrontation between them, so that the lack of consensus regarding the content of the "story" and the "we" telling it come to the fore (see also Goldstein 2004:17–18). Thus, as the Mexican case also suggests, soccer fandom, at least in intranational league competition, is less a conservative reflection of the way things are than a context where difference and often conflict are highlighted.

Whereas Bromberger et al.'s (1993) formulation relegates the team and its playing style to the realm of symbols, where their role is to represent something back in the "real" world of work and politics, Pumas fans in fact (and likely the fans of some other teams) rarely make such a distinction. While fans are quite aware, as Bromberger et al. suggest, that actual players and fans may not correspond to their ideal, this does not mean they are happy about it. It really matters to them how the Pumas players play and how their fellow fans cheer, and this is not just a concern with a representational "image."

Similarly, the application of performance theory to sporting events, following the seminal work of authors such as Turner (1982) and MacAloon, ed. (1984), produces interesting results, but is not necessarily applicable to all practices, or even the most significant ones, in the world of sports. In chapter 4, for example, I employ the concept of performance, but to analyze specific practices that I think my informants themselves would categorize in the same manner. However, it would be an overextension of the metaphor to apply the concept to the majority of their practices described here. The prominence of this framework in studies of sports fans is, I believe, rooted in a mind-body dichotomy basic to thinking in the modern Western world (Bell 1992) and motivated by the elite intellectual notion that what really count are the supposedly concrete, material realms of work and politics. At best, performances, spectacles, or rituals are treated as political tools for creating legitimacy (Handelman 1990; Goldstein 2004) and, at worst, as windows for studying how our informants view the "real" (Geertz 1973). However, this categorization as performance or as symbol leaves little room for treating fans' cheering practices as creative, engaging, concrete action constitutive of the material world.

The need to bridge the performance–real life dichotomy is heightened in this case by the postcolonial or neocolonial context. Mexico's two dominant collective imaginaries about the real life worlds of work and politics—clientelistic corporatism and neoliberal democracy (see below)—both lack legitimacy among a large proportion of urban residents who see them as either unrepresentative, unjust, or both. These imaginaries are hardly seen as models to reproduce in other areas of life. Instead, soccer fandom has become a space for developing and expressing alternatives and for negotiating confrontations between them. Thus, soccer fandom becomes a symbol, but not in the sense of something that reflects real life. Rather, it stands for other things in the sense that it is exemplary, leading the way instead of following. This is precisely what makes attention to soccer fandom in Mexico so important: it offers an opportunity to observe the everyday social dreams, projects, and divisions that are subsumed in Mexico's dominant collective imaginaries and overlooked in subtle ways by studies that begin and end with traditional sociological categories, such as class, civil society, and state, derived from the colonizers' societies.

My point is not that such categories are irrelevant to understanding these soccer fans, but rather that we need to pay attention to the manner in which actors adopt, question, and complicate them. My use of the terms "ideal vision" and "social project," instead of "collective imaginary" or some other alternative, is an effort to capture the fact that what my informants are doing is not reducible to symbolic performance. "Ideal vision" is meant to capture that they are not just seeing and describing what is around them but trying to imagine, in the full sense of the word, an alternative future. "Social project" conveys the fact that imagining an alternative future is just the first step in an effort to actually create it.

Soccer and Nation in the Americas

Studies of soccer and soccer fandom in Argentina are, not surprisingly, more attuned to the colonial dilemma of justifying independent nationhood through claims to both difference and competitiveness (Chatterjee 1986). These studies often explore the role that soccer itself played in the Argentinean state's struggle to create a national identity in contrast to the British neocolonizers of the early twentieth century (Archetti 1999; Alabarces 2002). According to Archetti (1999), soccer provided a context for Argentineans to beat the British at their own game and to do so through a distinctive Argentinean playing style. Again, soccer play was representative of Argentinean identity in an exemplary rather than a reflective sense: international soccer success would lead the way for other activities.

Although more research is needed on the connections between soccer and national identity in Mexico, I do not expect such research would uncover as significant a connection as in the Argentinean case. Mexico's neocolonial battles in the early twentieth century were fought on rural and agricultural instead of urban and industrial ground, as in Argentina. The Mexican Revolution was primarily a peasant struggle for land, and post-revolutionary portrayals of the nation focused on the value of the country's long-standing indigenous/peasant traditions. When international soccer competition began to grow in importance as the country rapidly industrialized and urbanized in the 1940s and 1950s, Mexico's principal national myths were already in place, leaving soccer out of the picture. Today Mexicans closely scrutinize the performance of the national team and of Mexican players in foreign leagues as measures of the country's international competitiveness, but the game still lacks the place in the national collective imaginary that it occupies in Argentina or Brazil.

This lack of a prominent national mythology regarding soccer, however, leaves more room for a plurality of soccer-based "ideal visions" within the country. Without a strong state presence in portrayals of soccer playing styles and fandom, Mexican fans are relatively free to imagine their ideal visions and social projects using the game, which is not to say that the nation is irrelevant to their visions and projects. The ideal visions of América, Chivas, Cruz Azul, and Pumas fans are inclusive at least up to the national level, meaning that they all propose futures for the country as a whole and not just for specific groups. As I have already suggested, these projects for the future make sense only in the context of a problematic present, to which I turn in the next section.

The Crumbling Pyramid: Contemporary Urban Mexican Sociality

In an influential article, the anthropologist Larissa Lomnitz initiated the somewhat daunting task of conceptualizing urban Mexican social structure, at a moment when it was dominated by corporate clientelism, by likening it to "a set of free-standing pyramids, each of which duplicates itself hierarchically like a crystal from top to bottom" (1982:52). According to Lomnitz, there are four of these free-standing pyramids: (1) the public sector, or government; (2) the labor sector; (3) the private sector; and (4) the informal or "popular" sector (1982:52). In my opinion, these pyramids are not always easy to distinguish, nor are they free standing. My concern here, however, is less with the content of the pyramids than with her description of their form and functioning. Lomnitz suggested that at the apex of each pyramid stands a national leader who exercises a sort of indirect rule, acting as a patron to and eliciting the loyalty of those immediately below him in the pyramid. The latter, in turn, act as patrons to those immediately below them and so on, so that each pyramid-shaped group of a patron and his clients replicates the whole structure on a reduced scale. Furthermore, all of the persons occupying the intermediary levels of the pyramid, in their dual roles as patrons to those below and clients to those above, act as power brokers "engaged in a permanent process of negotiation for [the downward flow of] resources in exchange for [the upward flow of] political support" (Lomnitz 1982:52). Successful performance, as a mediator in these vertical relationships, often depends on access to resources provided by horizontal relationships with friends and kin at the same level of the pyramid.

Lomnitz arrived at this model by allowing "the actors to describe the social structure through their own performance, and through the conceptualizations that they derive from their experiences within the system" (1982:51). In other words, it derives partially from her observations of people's performances but it is also a local, folk model that she borrowed from her informants. This methodology is significant in that it avoids the ethnocentric trap of beginning analysis with the European or North American assumption that social classes constitute the basis of the urban social structure. This is not to say that social classes are absent from urban Mexico, but that the pyramid's vertical ties, which bind actors from different classes and divide those from the same class, frequently override class-based loyalties. Lomnitz stated explicitly that her purpose was "not to deny the existence of conflict but to show how stability is maintained in spite of the enormous socioeconomic inequalities and contradictions within Mexican society" (1982:68). Her approach also avoided imposing the traditional categories "state" and "civil society" to a context where their use would create confusion, to say the least. The state's pyramidical corporate structure, extending throughout even the private sector, leaves little room for what we usually think of as civil society. If the state is all encompassing and conflated with society, then it also becomes difficult to apply this concept of "state" in the traditional sense.

Lomnitz's approach was innovative in that it applied anthropology's comparative method, concerned with cultural specificities and usually used in the analysis of rural, "traditional" societies, to the type of urban milieu often assumed to be European and "modern" in character. The fact that the model partially derives from people's own understandings of their social world is also significant because it means that the model itself is part of people's performances as it guides their actions, eliciting "responses of loyalty, competition, and patterns of exchange" (Lomnitz 1982:52). I would add that in an unintentional manner, this elicitation by the actors themselves functions as a sort of self-fulfilling prophecy: by acting to achieve success in the pyramid of corporate clientelism, people re-create and re-enforce it.

The anthropologist Carlos Vélez-Ibáñez added to Lomnitz's model process and the possibility of exclusion. Focusing on the early years of a squatter community of 500,000 people on the outskirts of Mexico City, Vélez-Ibáñez (1983) described the corporate state structure's failure to include the majority of the community's most needy in its pyramid of patron-client ties. In the late 1960s and early 1970s, residents, many of whom had only recently migrated from the countryside, organized to demand basic services such as water, drainage, and titles for their properties from the government. The government, however, instead of providing these services in exchange for loyalty, as would be expected in Lomnitz's model, countered residents' efforts by co-opting their leaders—drawing only *them* into the pyramidical structure—thereby weakening their organization and diminishing its effectiveness. Thus, while the movement resulted in substantial benefits for a privileged few, the vast majority ended up exactly where they had started, if not worse, because in the process they had lost their leaders, who had also been trusted friends. After experiencing a few rounds of this, residents realized that they were only wasting their time and they were better off preserving their solidarity and friendships even if they had no manner of producing effects beyond the community level. Vélez-Ibáñez called these series of events "rituals of marginality." The term "ritual" signals their processual and repetitive nature, whereas "marginality" refers to the fact that they end up reproducing the majority's exclusion from the state's distribution of benefits.

The present study builds on these two authors' efforts to conceptualize urban Mexico's social structure and sociality. As I suggested above, Pumas fans employ the idiom of soccer playing and cheering styles to conceptualize what they see as the positive and negative aspects of the social world around them. Following Lomnitz's methodology, I borrow my informants' models and combine them with my own observations of their practices to provide an ethnographically based conceptualization of aspects of urban Mexican social structure and sociality. One of the striking aspects of this conceptualization is its insistence on the coexistence of multiple models or modes of sociality. In fact, the models are always evoked in contrast to others. More specifically, these fans continually contrast the Pumas model of sociality, consisting of actions guided by heartfelt emotion, with the América model, in which all action depends on and derives from hierarchical relations to others—a close-up of Lomnitz's pyramid. The social models represented by the other two national teams, Chivas and Cruz Azul, allow for still other contrasts. This plurality clearly differs from Lomnitz's image of the stable and all-encompassing pyramid.

Vélez-Ibáñez's attention to marginality anticipates this plurality, particularly in his final ethnographic chapter, where he described residents becoming aware of not only the futility of making collective demands but also the existence and value of another type of social structure: the egalitarian relations of friendship, based on mutual assistance, that grew out of their shared experiences in rituals of marginality. Here I take up where Vélez-Ibáñez left off, focusing on the alternative social vision achieved through exclusion and on how this newly learned vision is used to challenge and even sometimes displace the pyramid and rituals of marginality. With no alternatives, actors' elicitation of the pyramid model can only be aimed to achieve success within it, because its existence is taken for granted. With alternative socialities, however, the potentialities of actors' own use of the models expands beyond the self-fulfilling prophecy. The elicitation of alternative models can serve as a critique of the status quo and bring about change. Thus, I observed how my informants draw contrasts between different modes of sociality with an eye to influencing how those around them relate to others and act in general.

The contrast between Lomnitz's static, unitary conceptualization and my own more processual, plural version stems both from differences in the kinds of actors we used as informants and the different moments at which the research was conducted in each case. Following the explanations provided by my own informants, their exclusion from the world of patron-client relations at work and in politics is due to their status as youths, who employers are reluctant to hire because they have not yet been transformed into passive clients. In contrast, although Lomnitz did not specify exactly who her informants were, they seem to be persons fully incorporated into one of the four pyramids. Furthermore, at the time Lomnitz wrote, even if the pyramids did not encompass all of Mexico City's residents (think of Vélez-Ibáñez's marginalized, for example), their reach was significant and in any case the perception of their omnipresence and stability was widely accepted. Beyond the more obvious—and in this system, integrated—spheres of work and politics, the corporatist structure even encompassed significant portions of what we usually refer to as civil society, such as neighborhood associations, student organizations, and other voluntary interest groups, thereby effectively blurring the line between state and civil society (Davis 1994:100–101). Personal relations entered the picture as well when actors brought in family members to work with or under them or such ties were created through ritual kinship (*padrinazgo* and *compadrazgo*). In these ways, the pyramid included many more people than even the formal structures of employment itself. The very image of the pyramid suggests how actors understood their social context as one of permanence and immensity, not to mention restriction and control.

The Mexican version of shifts to neoliberalism and flexible accumulation since the 1980s could be described as the crumbling of the pyramid, both as a description of social reality and as a model for actors' understanding of their social world. For many *capitalinos*, the shift to neoliberalism and flexible accumulation (Harvey 1990) has meant decreased job security and stability and at least a partial end to the network of social relations that previously were even more enduring than the jobs themselves. It makes little sense to maintain clientelistic relations in situations where there are no benefits to receive in downward exchanges and, in any case, the emergent labor relations and hiring practices are now demanding different strategies. Young people have often been hit hardest by this shift, because as the last hired, if hired at all, they were the easiest to exclude from the dwindling industrial and public sectors. Many of my informants are experiencing this exclusion as a disjuncture between what they had been prepared for through the education system and the reality they now face. As the Pumas fans themselves claim, they are able to develop their alternative, critical vision precisely because their exclusion from patron-client relations allows them to evade clientelistic subjectivity and thinking. Similarly, the weakening of these ties or the partial crumbling of the pyramid opens a space for the actual implementation of their alternative vision.

My preference for the term "sociality," by which I mean the specific manners in which people act through social relations and relate socially through actions, over Lomnitz's "social structure" is undoubtedly attributable to anthropology's shift over the past thirty years toward interest in actors and their actions. However, I think it also has something to do with changes in urban Mexico. Lomnitz's anthropological notion of "structure" was an appropriate match for urban Mexicans' understanding of their own social world in the 1970s. When I conducted my research in the late 1990s, however, actors were attuned to identifying different ways of being, relating and acting among people sitting right beside them in the stands during games, something the bulky concept of structure would have difficulty capturing.

Yet, other things have not really changed, such as the difficulty of applying the categories of state and civil society. Along these lines, I have struggled deciding how to appropriately categorize what exactly the fans of different teams and even the fans within the porra are battling over. On the one hand, the Pumas fans seem to be struggling against corporate clientelism for the existence of a civil society. However, if corporate clientelism extends beyond the state, then we need a broader term to talk about what the porra members are struggling against. The term "political culture" or Foucault's (1991) "governmentality" seem appropriate at first. They both span or ignore the state versus civil society divide, while capturing something important about what I describe here: politics in the broadest sense, that is, how power is distributed in society and how this distribution determines social relations, personhood, and action. Yet there is another problem. Although porra members are undoubtedly concerned with politics in this sense, they are quite clear that this is a means rather than an end in itself. Even their interest in the benefits of democracy, such as the freedom from clientelism promised by civil society, are just a means for achieving their real goal: the expression of heartfelt emotion. They resisted efforts aimed at fully democratizing the porra, or turning porra membership into citizenship.

In an attempt to take seriously their claim that their final goals have nothing to do with politics, I will resist using terms such as "political culture" or "governmentality" to categorize the struggle as a whole and terms such as "civil society" or "citizenship," which appear politically neutral only within the discourse of liberal democracy. I propose instead to talk about the overall struggle as being over "urban public sociality," because the struggle is generally limited to urban areas, and it is "public" in the sense that it is not directly about home life or family. In addition, this set of terms is applicable whether we are talking about civil society, citizenship, politics, or state. This is key because much of the struggle itself is about the extent and limits of modes of sociality associated with these categories and with other modes such as the one represented in the porra members' ideal vision. I recognize, however, that this set of terms is imperfect in the sense that the lines between public and private and between urban and rural are porous and shifting. Also, the categories are an imposition in that my informants do not speak in precisely these terms. In fact, they are not really concerned at all with categorizing or naming the overall struggle in which they take part. If anything, they would refer to it is as a struggle over how life should be lived. This offers me another tempting alternative, but I think that "urban public sociality" specifies that it is really only about some people's lives, some of the time.

Youth and Alternative Social Futures

The political freedom and economic exclusion resulting from neoliberal reforms have provoked searches for alternative manners of organizing society and defining citizenship, not just in Mexico but around the world, and particularly in developing regions (e.g., Holston 1999; Paley 2001; Gutmann 2002; Goldstein 2004). Young people seem to be playing a prominent role in these efforts (see Comaroff and Comaroff 1999; Diouf 1999; Cole 2004; Durham 2004; Verkaaik 2004), for basically the same reasons that Pumas fans see their youthfulness as significant: excluded from the usual positions of power in the public and private spheres, young people are both freer and more motivated to search for alternatives. Where the Pumas fans differ, perhaps, from the majority of these youth movements is the antipolitical nature of their proposed alternative. In this sense, they lie somewhere between these movements and what have been described as youth cultures concerned with style and difference (Hall and Jefferson, eds. 1976; Hebdige 1979), but not explicitly with politics. Compared to the latter, the Pumas fans appear more political, or at least more directed toward specific objectives and social alternatives, whereas in comparison with the former they are more concerned with creativity and expression. As I argue in the next chapter, close comparisons can be drawn between the Pumas fans' ideal vision and another movement that purposefully occupies this middle ground, although not usually considered a "youth culture": the Romantic artistic movement of the late eighteenth and earlier nineteenth centuries (see Talmon 1967).

Within urban Mexico there is overlap between students' political movements, both in terms of personnel and in styles of participation (see Carey 2005; Rodríguez Aguilar 2005), Pumas fandom, and certain rock music cultures (see Urteaga Castro-Pozo 1998; Zolov 1999). In student marches, participants chant cheers sung from the Pumas fans' repertoire and listen to rock music; Pumas fans rework popular rock songs into cheers; and Pumas fans' cheers and paraphernalia and rock cultures' songs and paraphernalia draw on popular political figures such as Che Guevara and el Subcomandante Marcos. However, there are also important differences among these three youth cultures, once again with the Pumas fans laying somewhere in the middle. Pumas fans are careful to distinguish their practices from the directly political nature of student movements, emphasizing instead bodily, emotional expression that rock music cultures also share. Although Pumas fans are not openly concerned with distinguishing themselves from rock fans, an important difference between the two stems from the fact that the competitive nature of soccer requires a common ground—the "grounds," literally, and the game itself—and forces constant public confrontation over that common ground. This confrontation, especially in the case of the four national teams, encourages the development and promotion of ideal visions for the future of common grounds, including soccer and, by metaphoric extension, society as a whole. In contrast, rock subcultures lack such institutionalized public confrontation. They tend to be inward-looking and to isolate their followers, thereby discouraging such attention to common grounds that the four national teams' fans and political movements share.

Although Pumas fans explicitly use the notion of youth to identify themselves and their perspective on life, this identification is once again a means to an end and not an end itself. Porra members are clear that their youthfulness, with its exclusion and thus freedom, makes them the appropriate flag bearers of a social project that concerns not just young people but all Mexicans or even all humans. There is no fetishization of youth or wish to "die before they get old," as can often be found in rock music, for example. The open-endedness of the project appears to be another product of soccer's competition over common grounds. According to porra members, old people tend to act differently, although this is not necessarily the case, just as young people can be América fans. This thinking also explains their lack of concern over the actual ages of players despite the team's motto of puros jóvenes: their preoccupation is with a specific style of play associated with youthfulness. It could be said that youth stands for their idea of how soccer should be played and for their social project, but what really matters to them are the play and the project, not youthfulness itself. I resist making youth my primary category of analysis to remain faithful to my informants' own interests and understandings of themselves.

Still another version of youthfulness present here and in most of the studies cited above is the common idea of young people, and in particular young men, as disorderly and dangerous. The Mexican case presents its own particular version of this idea, which I introduce briefly in the next section and elaborate upon in chapter 4.

Masculinity, Disorder, Violence

Various authors have treated contemporary urban Mexican masculinity and gender relations in the context of marriage, home, and family (Benería and Roldán 1992; González de la

Rocha 1994; Gutmann 1996; Brandes 2002; Magazine 2004a). While urban Mexican masculinity and gender relations in public contexts have received some attention from historians (O'Malley 1986; Zolov 1999; Carey 2005), we still have few contemporary data based on empirical research. Instead, we have stereotypical images derived from national myths regarding the typical urban Mexican man. Mexican intellectuals first created such myths during the period of political instability following the revolution. Their images of working-class urban Mexican men as angry and violent but disorganized served to legitimate paternalistic state rule while denying a serious threat to public security (O'Malley 1986; Bartra 1987). A new period of political uncertainty brought on by neoliberal reforms and the crumbling of the pyramid have led intellectuals to bring back such images (Monsiváis 1995; C. Lomnitz 1996; Zermeño 1996; Bartra 1998). Their recent portrayals of young urban men as stuck between old and new manners of organizing society are then circulated in the media and subsequently adopted in different manners by urban residents. The frequent use of *el desmadre* (disorder; literally motherlessness) to describe young men's actions, which I elaborate upon in chapter 4, reflects this kind of portrayal.

Pumas fans, and more specifically porra members, are frequently portrayed as young men who are angry because of their political and economic exclusion and who channel this anger into random, meaningless acts of violence because they lack the guidance to do anything else. Due to these images, many people consider the stadium a dangerous place to go, but at the same time do not see these young men as a serious threat to social order and security precisely because of their supposed disorganization. On the positive side, this kind of portrayal has meant that the porra members' playful and not so playful violent behavior does not meet with the kind of serious reprisals from police that fans in other countries, such as England and Argentina, have had to face (see Archetti and Romero 1994; Armstrong 1998). On the negative side, however, these portrayals obscure the porra members' and other Pumas fans' more complex and, in fact, quite well thought out ideas about what it means to be a young man in contemporary urban Mexico and what might be done to improve their lot and that of others. In chapter 4, I discuss how porra members manipulate and sometimes adopt these images derived from national myths. Meanwhile, the other ethnographic chapters constitute an effort to see beyond such myths to how the porra members—as youths, as men, and as Mexicans—conceptualize the world around them and attempt to transform it.

The Team and Its Fans

The Pumas

The Pumas' philosophy of puros jóvenes or *darles chance a los jóvenes* (to give young players a chance) was brought to the Pumas in the early 1960s by an Argentine coach and former player, Renato Cesarini. Cesarini brought from Argentina the notion that the best soccer is not found in mature, older players, but in the undisciplined, creative style of *el pibe*. In one version of Argentina's unofficial national mythology, el pibe is the boy who grows up playing soccer in "empty and uneven urban spaces—without any teachers, unlike in England where . . . [soccer] was integral to the school system" (Archetti 1999:180). In the absence of school discipline and unbound by the responsibilities of adulthood, el pibe is free to develop a typically Argentine style of play characterized by improvisation, imagination, and spontaneity (Archetti 1999:180) in contrast to the disciplined, collective, powerful, and "machine-like" British style (1999:60). Cesarini also believed that players brought up with the team would be more loyal and dedicated to it (Eduardo Archetti, personal communication). He established the current structure of the Pumas by setting up Mexico's first *fuerzas básicas* (basic forces), a youth league run by the team to develop new talent and feed the professional team. Cesarini's efforts exemplify the tension between modernity and the ideal of authentic heartfelt expression. Having grown up playing soccer himself, Cesarini valued el pibe's style of play in and of itself, but as a coach he saw it as a means to win games. Although the connection between soccer and the ideal of authentic heartfelt expression seen in Mexico did not originate in Argentina, Cesarini and the Argentine myth he brought with him clearly played essential roles in the establishment in Mexico of an institutional basis for the connection.

Fans of other Mexican teams value the puros jóvenes philosophy because they consider las fuerzas básicas and the Pumas team to be the training grounds for the country's best players, analogous to the UNAM's role in the scientific-bureaucratic training of the country's leaders.[6] For porra members, while the Pumas' role in supplying talent to other teams may be a source of pride, the philosophy of puros jóvenes is not just a means to an end but an end in itself, because the players' youthfulness is the key to their heartfelt, creative, and passionate play.

Besides the fuerzas básicas, the other distinctive feature of the team's organizational structure is its ownership. When the team first joined the Mexican soccer league in the early 1960s, it was an amateur team that drew its players entirely from the student body of the UNAM. In the early 1970s, to compete in the improving league, the team began paying its players and eliminated the requirement that players be students at the university. To protect the UNAM from possible financial loss, a group of alumni formed a not-for-profit corporation that would sponsor and administer the team. The corporation directs profits from ticket sales and television contracts back to the team and the university, while the alumni on the board of directors absorb any financial losses incurred by the corporation. The Pumas is the only team in the Mexican First Division soccer league administered in this manner. Despite the fact that now few players study at the UNAM, there remains a strong link between the Pumas and la máxima casa de estudios (the highest house of learning) as it is often called. For example, the university's anthem is played over the loudspeakers before the start of every game and serious fans know the words and sing along whether or not they have actually studied there. Further, the team plays its home games and trains in the stadium officially called El Estadio Olímpico Universitario (The Olympic University Stadium)[7] and commonly known as CU, short for Ciudad Universitaria (University City), because of its location on the enormous campus with over 100,000 students in the southern part of Mexico City.

The Porra Plus and Its Members

The Pumas team counts thousands of supporters who regularly attend its home games. Hundreds of thousands more throughout Mexico City and the rest of the country claim fan status even without regular visits to the stadium. However, because my research is ethnographic, I focused on one group of fans, organized into what is referred to locally as a porra, or what we might call a fan club or cheering group. When I began my research, there were two porras supporting the Pumas, the Ultra and the Plus,[8] and I ended up focusing on the second, which was the larger and more prominent of the two. The Porra Plus counts about 100 members, most of whom are males between the ages of sixteen and thirty. It also includes a few wives, girlfriends, sisters, and children of the young men, a small number of single young women, and a few older male members.

Although the Pumas' fan base is not limited to particular parts of the city or a particular social class, most porra members live in one of two sections of the city, each of which houses residents of a particular class background. About half of them live in the southern section of the city, which middle- and upper-class residents began to occupy in the 1950s to escape the "immoral" practices of their working-class neighbors in the center (Rubenstein 2001:222–24). Most of their parents have university degrees and white-collar jobs, often in the government bureaucracy. They themselves attend or have attended one of the public high schools administered by the UNAM, and many go on to study at the university itself. The middle-class residents of the south are already generally familiar with the sort of social critique that constitutes the porra members' outlook when they join the group. It could be said that it comes naturally to them or that the residents of the south are the unnamed source of the porra's ideal vision.

While a few club members come from the industrial northern part of the city, almost half come from the eastern quarter, which is more difficult to categorize in terms of class. Not middle class like the south or consistently and explicitly industrial and working class like the north, the porra members from the east are the class-ambiguous or class-mobile "everyone else" whose parents work as handymen, artisans, and small business owners.[9] While many of these families from this part of the city have achieved middle-class status in an economic sense, sometimes with higher incomes than porra members' families from the south, the porra members' generation is the first to aspire to and begin to achieve middle-class status in a cultural and socially recognizable sense, often through attending the UNAM or one of its high schools. Nevertheless, most of the club members from the east combine their studies with part-time or full-time work, primarily as cashiers and clerks, and others work full-time and speak of plans to return to school. Because residents from the east often encounter the porra's critical position later in life, they are open to accusations of inauthentically performing the critique rather than truly feeling it. They have a more ambiguous relationship to the group's critical stance because their support of it can be interpreted positively as an end in itself or negatively as a means to achieve an appearance of middle-class status.

Members from all parts of the city deny any link between their fandom and either class or residency and instead account for their common allegiance to the Pumas, a cheering style, and a particular worldview in terms of the age category *jóvenes* (youths). In fact, they state that they are drawn to the Pumas because the team's young players share their experiences and outlook on life. Porra members explain that employers refuse to hire them, just like other teams would bypass the young Pumas players, because their skills and abilities are unproven and, more importantly, they have not yet been transformed into passive, uncritical clients who are easier for employers to control and exploit.

Although their complaint of exclusion can be heard among young people around the world, it should be noted that the cohort under study came of age at a moment in Mexican history when a middle class that had been growing for forty years began to shrink. Between the 1940s and the 1980s, Mexico's "economic miracle" saw the children of workers and petty merchants experience a rate of upward social mobility into white-collar, middle-class jobs even greater than that of economic growth itself (Escobar Latapí and Roberts 1991:101). A policy of import substitution aimed at strengthening a highly centralized, nationally based economy concentrated this upward mobility in Mexico City. To meet employers' demands for trained workers and people's demand for access to the new jobs, the government expanded public university education during the 1960s and 1970s. Beginning in the 1980s, however, economic crises, along with the neoliberal economic policies implemented to resolve them, caused Mexico City's white-collar job market to collapse even as public universities continued to train large numbers of students for these jobs. The economic downturn left many of the porra members from the south with little hope of maintaining their parents' middle-class status and left many of those from the east with little hope of achieving their parents' middle-class aspirations. Many from both areas are in limbo, frustrated and suspended indefinitely between school and work, childhood and adulthood. Although the end of upward social mobility and the beginning of downward mobility does describe the situation faced by many, and they themselves often emphasize this aspect of their common lot in their self-representations as jóvenes, the extent of this dire state should not be exaggerated. Some study at the UNAM and maintain hopes of finding stable white-collar jobs, and others have already left school and found those jobs. Meanwhile, there are also a few members who never had middle-class aspiration and who work as bodyguards, waiters, and at other unskilled, nonindustrial jobs.

Considering the porra members' self-proclaimed economic plight, it would not be surprising to find their critique of clientelism and modernity-as-end directed toward the problem of socioeconomic inequality. Yet, they insist that their occupational exclusion as jóvenes is significant to them not for economic or political reasons, but because it leaves them free from the stifling effects of modernity and clientelism. This, in turn, allows them to see these social arrangements critically and to value the fulfillment of authentic heartfelt desire over progress, materialism, and clientelistic power. They claim that their actions are still guided by that which is basically and inherently human— their inner emotions—because they and the players, as youths, have not yet been transformed by external influences including clientelism and scientific objectivity or democratic rationality. Without these external influences that come to dominate and dull older people after they have spent time in the world of work and politics, they are free to experience genuine emotion such as love, passion, or joy. Thus, their practices on the field, in the stands, or in life in general are guided from within and not by dependence on others, as in clientelism, nor by external objective rules or logic, as in democracy or the free market.

A key personality in the porra is its president, Ernesto, a middle-aged lawyer. Ernesto was elected the first president of the porra in early 1995 after the group's previous and only other leader in its eight-year history, Javier, stopped attending the games. Porra members describe Javier as an authoritarian and charismatic figure whom they never thought to question. Ernesto contrasts himself with Javier by claiming that his goal is to make the porra more democratic. For example, he insists that the members elect the president and all other positions such as treasurer and cheer leader, that members make important decision as a group during meetings, and that membership in the club and, in particular, access to free tickets donated by the team, be determined on the rational basis of numbers of games missed and attended. This shift from the authoritarianism of the old leader to Ernesto's democracy parallels a simultaneous shift in Mexican politics at the national level.

While porra members recognize that much of their critical perspective developed thanks to Ernesto's democratic freedom, they do not hesitate to turn their critical gaze back upon him. For example, they state that the requirements for membership cannot be quantified. Instead, they claim that when a fan is allowed or asked to join and sit with the group, it should be because he shares a genuine love for the team and all it stands for. In other words, they believe that they can sense whether a fan possesses the proper criteria for membership, but that these criteria cannot be measured. Furthermore, they say that their critical perspective allows them to see that Ernesto's democracy is often no more than a thin veil for continuing clientelism. They point out, for example, that Ernesto often takes on the role of *cacique* (power broker), mediating between the porra members and the team management. Through Ernesto, the team management provides a limited number of free tickets to games, some funding for trips to away games, and permission to mark off a section of the stadium for porra seating. In exchange, the team management wants Ernesto to discipline the young club members so that they eliminate bad language and roughhousing from their cheering, which, it claims, keeps families away from the stadium and reduces ticket sales. My informants claim that instead of distributing the free tickets rationally, Ernesto gives them to members in exchange for their loyalty and obedience, helping him to comply with the team's wishes and maintain his clientelistic exchanges with the team. While their criticism of Ernesto and the alternatives they propose are illustrative of their critical stand, the fact that some members enter into clientelistic exchanges with him shows that even within the club, members' practices are not as consistently anticlientelistic as their self-representation would suggest.

The Research

As often occurs with anthropological field research, my selection of the Pumas and the Porra Plus as research topics was somewhat serendipitous. I arrived in Mexico City in late November 1995 to study the effects of NAFTA on soccer in Mexico. In particular, I was interested in how the opening of the Mexican market to U.S. corporations might affect Mexican soccer through a process of accelerated commodification. In fact, I did find something of the sort in connection with the Pumas and its fans, but my focus had by then shifted. In an attempt to get started by meeting some soccer fans, I visited a public *deportivo* (a recreation center) near the city center. Because my first visits were over the Christmas holidays, the center was almost empty except for the participants in a government program for *los niños de la calle* (street children). The so-called street children, who were not so childlike in appearance or even in age, turned into another research topic (see Magazine 2000, 2003b, 2004a). One of them also turned into my unlikely guide into the world of soccer supporters and, more specifically, the Pumas. I say unlikely because twenty-two-year-old Jorge was unique among the street children both because of his regular attendance at professional games and because he was a Pumas fan. Most of his peers rarely had the money or made the effort to attend games, and the teams they followed on television or in the newspapers were primarily América and Cruz Azul. After hearing of my interest in soccer fans, Jorge proclaimed that it was my lucky day because not only had I encountered a genuine fan, but also a member of best porra in all of Mexico.

A couple of weeks later we attended a game together. All of the porra members he introduced me to greeted me warmly, but a few minutes before halftime one member sitting near the front of the group's section turned and started yelling that if I did not start supporting the team, they would throw me out of the section. At halftime, my accuser approached to confront me, but when Jorge explained that I was a friend of his and a foreigner who did not know the cheers, his attitude changed and he welcomed me. I think that my foreignness was a key to my rapid acceptance in the group, whose members were usually quite strict regarding who could and could not sit with them in the section. Their objective, as I came to understand later, was distinguishing authentic from inauthentic Pumas fans, and their main concern was weeding out those who were really Americanistas—in the sense of a personality type—even if the fan himself did not know it. As a foreigner and despite my status as a potentially imperialist American, my lack of Pumas-like passionate expression indicated ignorance and inability rather than inauthenticity. My ignorance did not exempt me from occasional teasing, but I was able to join the group and begin to conduct my research as a participant-observer.

From early 1996 through May 1997 I attended all of the Pumas home games as a member of the porra. I also went to the team's away games that the porra attended as a group. The third of the away games played against teams in the city or its outskirts were easy and inexpensive for group members to attend. Another third, within a four- or five-hour drive from the capital, drew reduced numbers: usually one busload. The third of away games I did not attend were considered too far and costly to travel to by most. Often I watched these games on television with one or more porra members. Attending games involved far more than the two-hour match. For the usual Sunday home games at noon, porra members started gathering at the stadium at nine o'clock, which for most meant leaving home an hour or more before and riding at least one subway line and one bus to get to the stadium. Porra members arrived early to put their names on a list for discounted tickets, but they also used the three hours in the parking lot to greet and *cotorrear con* (joke around with) the other porra members, many of whom they only saw once a week. For me it was also an ideal time to participate in and listen to their conversations, because during the game most of their attention was directed toward their cheering.

During the games, I cheered along with the group once I

learned the words to the cheers and songs, while trying to observe and understand what was going on around me and on the field. Also, with time, the cheering came to really mean something for me. I attribute my fandom not just to familiarity—that I happened to be going to Pumas games and not those of some other team—but also to a partial match between the Pumas fans' ideal vision and my own. Here, though, I think that what allowed me to enter the porra so easily, my foreignness, was also a limiting factor in my becoming a fan and the reason why the fit was only partial. The Pumas fans' ideal vision really only makes full sense in relation or opposition to other such visions found in urban Mexican society. I could come to understand the subtleties of the Pumas fans' ideal vision in a cerebral manner through research, but, not having grown up in Mexico, I did not really feel the love for the Pumas and hate for the others with the intensity my informants did.

In the stadium, the porra members tended to sit in the same part of the group's section and with the same fellow members every game. To make my research a study of the whole porra and not just a few members, I made an effort to vary my seating location. Nevertheless, I sat in one area most frequently and with the same group of five or six porra members, who were also my best informants and closest friends. Most anthropologists who have done fieldwork are familiar with the kind of depth versus breadth decision I was faced with in the porra. They will also know, however, that more often than not the course our research takes has less to do with rational decision-making than with at least three other factors. First, our informants end up choosing us at least as often as we choose them. Second, our own and our informants' desires to create close friendships may tip the scales toward depth. Finally, when divisions and conflicts arise it is difficult to split our loyalties without potentially alienating both sides. Therefore, when conflicts arose in the porra, even while I avoided participating openly, just the fact of who I was standing close to created an appearance of partisanship and limited who would or would not take me into their full confidence.

After home games we would retire to the same section of the parking lot occupied before the game. I participated in postgame activities including pick-up soccer games, drinking, and more *cotorreo* (joking around). These activities lasted until about five or six o'clock, when most of the porra members had already left and those remaining resigned themselves to ending the day's fun and going home. My final phase of participant-observation for the day consisted of riding the bus and subway toward our homes with the last group of porra members to leave the stadium. This travel was usually slow. The porra members were in no hurry to get home, and they paused frequently during the trip to continue joking around or discussing the day's events in the stands and on the field. I think that porra members tried to extend this time with these friends as much as possible, because their dispersion throughout the city made it difficult to socialize more often. The fact that this socializing took place in parking lots and subway stations was hardly a deterrent, because for these young men who lived with their parents and did not have the money to spend in restaurants or bars, there were really no other options. This extended gathering, but also our dwindling numbers both in the parking lot and then on public transportation, provided me with the opportunity to have more private and personal discussions with smaller groups of porra members. During these discussions I could ask them for explanations and actually expect more serious, thoughtful answers, which would have resulted in teasing for their seriousness earlier in the day. On these occasions, I would ask them, for example, to elaborate on the distinctions they drew between different types of players, fans, and people in general and their comportment both inside and outside the stadium. My questions would often provoke further discussion among my informants as they disagreed with, corrected, and bettered each others' theories.

My observation on days of away games outside the city usually began at four or five o'clock in the morning, when we met at a designated spot to board the bus for the four- or five-hour trip to our destination. This early-morning trip was an ideal opportunity to observe the porra members' performance of el desmadre, hyped-up as they were for the trip and with the perfect unsuspecting audience in passersby both as we left the capital and entered the opponent's city. The games themselves provided a chance to observe a direct interaction between the porra and fans from outside Mexico City, an interaction that was distinct from that between Pumas fans and fans of the capital's other teams. For the opposing fans, the Pumas supporters represented the capital as a whole and its exploitation of the rest of the country under a highly centralized state, even more than a specific Pumas philosophy. During the trip home, the desmadre continued but in a subdued manner with everyone tired out by the day's activities. This calmer period, with my informants trapped on the bus, provided me with another good opportunity to have serious discussions.

Between games, I participated in various activities with porra members, including parties in their homes, gatherings outside the stadium to paint banners, and pick-up or more organized soccer games. It was between games that I conducted interviews with porra members. I would approach a porra member after the game and ask if he or she would be willing to be interviewed, and then we would plan to meet either at their home, mine, their place of work, or a public place such as a restaurant or park. In total, I conducted and tape-recorded more than forty such interviews. I tried to interview a wide range of porra members, including young men from various subgroups, the porra's president, a couple of other older members, and a few of the women. During interviews, I gathered basic information regarding where and with whom they lived and their work and educational activities. I then interviewed them about a number of topics, including how they came to be Pumas fans and porra members, the significance of el desmadre, relationships between men and women in public and private contexts, and the problems with the porra and how they might be corrected. The interviews also provided me the opportunity to observe and interact with porra members in a situation apart from the porra and the stadium.

Visits to their houses and workplaces gave me a better idea of how they lived and worked. In fact, these interviews were among the few occasions I had to observe and interact with porra members in such contexts.

My lack of participant observation of porra members' daily lives undoubtedly constitutes a limitation to this study. Anthropologists are drawn to this kind of holistic data collection because it allows us to locate and make sense of our particular object of study in the wider context of people's lives. Because our unit of analysis extends to include all aspects of people's lives, everything they do is data, and a key datum is as likely to appear when we are not even looking for it—during a conversation over breakfast, for example—as during an interview. While conscious of this limitation during my research, I failed to come up with a way to get around it. My informants' homes were spread throughout a gigantic city, so that there was no residential community of the sort that allows anthropologists to live with or near all of their research subjects. I could have tried to live with or near one porra member or to divide my time living with or near two or three. However, because of their diversity in terms of class background, neighborhoods, educational levels, and occupations, it seemed that data collected in so few households would hardly be representative. Obviously, this is a problem faced by most anthropologists trying to conduct research in large cities or it at least explains why many decide to focus their studies on places of residence such as neighborhoods, leaving many other residentially dispersed urban social phenomena unstudied. My own anthropological craving for at least some sort of community, fixed in space and membership, explains my focus on the porra and not on Pumas fans in general.

After leaving Mexico City in May 1997, I returned for visits in January, March, and July 1998. During my first visit I did not have the opportunity to attend any games, but I spoke with porra members who told me about the radical changes in the porra that had occurred since I had left. During my second and third visits of 1998, I attended home games and observed the changes first hand. In August 1998 I also had the opportunity to interview a few porra members about these changes, which I describe in chapter 6. By September 1999, I was once again living in Mexico City. While new family and work obligations made it difficult to continue attending games and meeting with porra members during the week, I had the opportunity to follow the Pumas and the porra on television and in the newspapers—the porra tends to attract a lot of attention from television cameras and sportswriters' pens.

In May 2004, inspired by the Pumas' victory in the spring 2004 tournament, I renewed contact with informants, who once again recounted significant changes in the porra. I attended a game in August 2004 to observe these changes first hand and then continued to meet with these same fans more regularly during the rest of the year, often to watch the team's away games on television. During these meetings, our discussions focused on transformations that had occurred during the last few years related to the porra, to Pumas supporters beyond the porra, and even to Mexican soccer fandom in general. The research conducted in 2004 also gave me the chance to observe and participate in Pumas fans' celebration of the team's championship victories in the spring of 2004 and then again in the fall—something I did not have the opportunity to learn from and enjoy during any of the other seasons since beginning my fieldwork in January 1996.

An Overview

In the next chapter, I illustrate how porra members articulate their ideal vision and their critique of other modes of public sociality through the idioms of soccer playing and cheering styles. Briefly, an attacking instead of a defensive style of play and proactive instead of reactive cheering represent the difference between the Pumas fans' allegiance to genuine heartfelt emotional expression versus other fans' clientelistic or overly rationalized practices. The group members' elaborate critical conceptualization of clientelism is particularly notable. Drawing on metaphors such as *el consentido* (the spoiled child) and *la mafia*, it contributes a unique subaltern understanding of this mode of sociality, positing that the world of work and politics creates "clientelized" subjects incapable of critical thought and heartfelt emotional expression. They claim that as youths, who have not yet been clientelized in this manner, they are in an ideal position to act as the flag bearers of passionate emotional expression, not just for other young people but for society as a whole. I conclude the chapter by drawing a comparison between this ideal vision and the Romantic artistic movement, arguing that like late eighteenth- and early nineteenth-century Romanticism, the emergence of the porra's alternative social project is closely connected to ambiguous and shifting political and economic conditions at national and global levels.

In chapter 3, I provide an ethnographic account of how the porra members put their alternative social project into practice during a typical game day. The action begins as the fans meet in the parking lot hours before the game, greeting each other and imposing a separation between the ambiguities of daily life and the supposedly pure Pumas sociality that is about to start. Once in the stadium, however, a conflict materializes between the young porra members and the group's president. What appears at first to be a conflict over cheering styles is also a struggle over control of the group and the social form it should take. The president attempts to impose precisely what the young group members most despise: a hierarchical group organization built upon clientelistic relations and thinly veiled by democratic rhetoric. This social order facilitates a cheering style in which group members simply follow the president's lead. The young men, however, resist this order and cheering style by breaking spontaneously in songs, which quickly catch on among their peers. This confrontation in the stands, leading to ever-increasing tensions within the group, reflects struggles over public sociality in Mexico City more generally, at a moment when neoliberal reforms continue to weaken the bonds of clientelism.

Another conflict emerges during game days between the group's few female members and the male majority. These young women have a somewhat different idea of what it means to support the team that includes forming—or at least imagining—personal relationships with the players. The male porra members are highly critical of this as well as of romantic relationships within the group and even of close dyadic friendships between men. I interpret this criticism as an externalization of the young men's internal conflict between their own attractions to dyadic friendships and romantic/domestic relationships versus their loyalty to the group and its ideals. I relate these findings to other public contexts in Mexico where women come to represent the threat posed by men's own interests in the domestic sphere.

Chapter 4 offers an ethnographic account of the playful (but often violent and sexually aggressive) practices that porra members refer to as el desmadre. I try to make sense of these practices by placing them in the framework of conflicts within the group and in the broader context of meanings of violence, disorder, and masculinity derived from a series of national myths about the typical urban Mexican man. In recent years, as during other periods of political and economic transition and uncertainty, Mexican intellectuals have invented a tradition of a disorderly, violent, but relatively harmless young urban man in need of a more stable political structure's control and guidance. In this chapter, I take a different approach, focusing on how the young fans both blindly follow and consciously manipulate these invented traditions. This leads to an account of masculinity and gender relations in public spaces that includes both the porra member's abuse of women as well as their performance of this typical male role to provoke reactions of fear or anger among observers. This type of performance is particularly evident in trips to away games, when the porra members provokingly enact the role of Mexico City residents arriving to supposedly lead, but in reality to exploit, their provincial compatriots. I demonstrate how the porra members use these performances of el desmadre to provoke a paternalistic reaction in the group's president, thereby distracting his attention from their serious objective of taking control of and transforming the group.

In chapter 5, I move from the ethnographic present to a narrative style, in an attempt to portray the porra as a process of domination, struggle, and innovation through which the porra members refined and then attempted to put into action their ideal vision. I suggest that the group's various transformations—from authoritarian rule to incomplete democratization to the emergence of an alternative form of organization—parallel transformations in Mexican urban society more generally, providing a window for viewing and understanding such processes. Over the course of my research, I observed how porra members became aware of various conflicting interests, including the team management's desire to pacify them, Nike's wish to commodify the group, and the president's hopes of benefiting as a middleman. Their awareness of these diverse interests led them to clarify and push forward their own interests. In response, the president began implementing a series of strategies meant to stifle the porra members' efforts. Once again, I observed the growth of the porra members' awareness, followed this time by the emergence of counter-strategies of resistance. The narrative reaches a point of crisis at a group meeting when the young porra members attempted to oust the president. When this failed, another lesson had been learned: confronting the president directly would only lead to humiliation or to losing leaders through co-optation. At this point the porra members began to withdraw their resistance and to search for other alternatives (a process I describe in chapter 6). This processual view of the group serves as a reminder that what looks like stable organizational or group "structure" to an outside observer may in fact constitute just one moment in a process of change.

In chapter 6, I present findings from follow-up research, which revealed a continuation of the process described in chapter 5, characterized first by the founding of a new porra, dubbed La Rebel, dedicated specifically to the implementation of the young porra members' ideal vision, then by this new group's rapid growth, and finally by its return to the sort of clientelistic relations its founders claimed to so despise. I also show how the prominence of this new group resulted in the diffusion of its cheering style, first to other Pumas fans and then to the fans of other teams, resulting in a "Rebelization" of the Pumas and a "Puma-ization" of Mexican soccer fandom. This diffusion is the local continuation of a process of globalization in which South American and European cheering styles were first adopted by porra members, who admired these other fans' passionate support of their teams.

In conclusion, I reiterate my argument that in the partial social and political vacuum created by neoliberalism and the crumbling of the corporatist pyramid, latent social projects, such as that of the porra members, have come to the fore to compete with clientelism and liberal democracy over the shape and texture of urban public sociality. However, the porra members' case suggests the need to take seriously the neoliberal project's successes. Their ideal vision, for example, with its call for an inner rather than an external motivation for action, approaches the liberal ideal of the self-governing person. The match is not perfect, however, and their social project does provide some real alternatives—not just to neoliberalism, but to all sociopolitical systems that define work and politics as ends in themselves rather than the means to a better life.

2

Being Puma

Life as Passionate Heartfelt Expression

Daniel, a twenty-five-year-old office clerk who lives in Mexico City, explained why he cheers for the Pumas by associating opposing teams' styles of play with political corruption:

> The Pumas play more forward. Even if they're winning they always take risks. They play an open style of soccer. The other teams are *ratoneros* [literally mice-catchers; meaning someone playing the waiting game of a cat trying to lure a mouse]. They are mediocre because they only play for the counter attack. With [the other teams], you do what you're told and that's a way of humiliating yourself, making yourself less than you are. Being a Pumas fan is a way of staying out of that atmosphere. Everything else is controlled by the government and by personal interests. I want to distance myself from this *suciedad* [filth]. [1]

Daniel, like the other members of the Porra Plus, claims that the only way to avoid the mediocre performance intrinsic to corruption is to distance oneself from it, because it pervades and transforms everything it contacts.

Through this and other such explanations, I became familiar with the porra members' elaborate critical conceptualization, phrased in the idiom of soccer playing and cheering styles, of what scholars refer to as clientelism. The porra members draw an analogy between the playing and cheering styles of rival teams and fans versus the deferential and passive approach to life engendered by the clientelistic relationships that they claim pervade Mexican society. They suggest that clientelistic relations transform the subjective orientations of potential clients, thereby determining and limiting how they approach social relations and practices. Conversely, the porra members claim that because the Pumas players and they themselves are excluded from clientelistic relations due to their youth, their play and cheering are inspired by heartfelt love for the game of soccer, the Pumas, and life in general. They assert that this heartfelt inspiration finds expression in spontaneous, passionate, and creative playing and cheering styles.

The porra members claim to be struggling against clientelism to achieve egalitarian friendship as well as passion, spontaneity, joy, and creativity. They add, moreover, that certain aspects of modernity such as democracy and liberalism are as threatening to their objectives as clientelism. According to group members, soccer play and cheering can be passionate, spontaneous, joyous, and creative only if they emerge from within the individual player or fan, *del corazón* (from the heart). They propose that external influences guiding soccer play and cheering, including the rationality and materialism of modernity as well as clientelism in the case of modernity's failure, stifle the universal human potential for authentic heartfelt expression. Although they reject aspects of modernity along with clientelism, they recognize that their position would not be imaginable without modernity's criticality, freedom, and equality. According to the club's members, while the democratization of the porra and of Mexico in general allows them to openly oppose clientelism, their ultimate objective is not democracy, criticality, freedom, or equality in themselves, but rather heartfelt expression through cheering. Thus, their stance is made possible by modernity-as-means: modernity in its liberating and critical form, which enables release from clientelism and other kinds of authoritarianism. Their stance also rejects modernity-as-end: modernity in the form of progress, in which rationality, objectivity, and the free market come to be seen as ends in themselves.[2] In other words, they claim that soccer should not be used to showcase scientific or technological progress, increase profits, or reproduce clientelistic hierarchies, because passionate, spontaneous, creative, and beautiful soccer play is an end in itself. For the porra members, soccer playing and cheering styles constitute the basis for a supra-ideological social commentary, meant as a reminder that political ideology, including modern democracy, is a means to an end and not an end in itself.

Soccer is particularly well suited to represent the tensions among clientelism, modernity-as-end, and the porra members' ideal of critical "heartfelt" expression. The rules of soccer parallel the democracy of modernity-as-means, protecting the freedom and equality of the players and thus allowing for individual creative expression. In addition, soccer is a competition with winners and losers. Winning may be perceived as a reflection of the triumph of creative expression. Yet winning can also be seen as an end in itself for which individuals must channel their creative expression to fit a rationalized team system that in turn leads to victories. Furthermore, players' relative freedom on the field allows for the pursuit of more personal interests such as individual clientelistic success. Although it is impossible to identify an action on the field or in the stands as authentically and wholly modern, clientelistic, or heartfelt, discourses of soccer playing and cheering styles provide concrete bodily idioms for representing these three positions and the tensions among them.

As will become apparent in subsequent chapters, the porra members, like most other Mexico City residents, alternately and simultaneously pursue clientelistic, modern, and heartfelt ends. They use patron-client ties and study accounting and engineering, for example, to get jobs. What distinguishes them is not their avoidance of clientelism and rationalism—a feat difficult to imagine for anyone in present-day Mexico—but rather their self-representation as the flag bearers of a critical stance struggling to keep two more dominant positions, modernity-as-end and clientelism, in check. Their highly coherent representation of this position is only imaginable as an abstraction from the complex and incessant flow of social life, including soccer games.

Soccer Playing Styles and Clientelism

Porra members state that they are drawn to the Pumas team by its attacking style of play, which contrasts with the defensive style of the rest of the teams in the league. In the game of soccer more generally, an attacking style refers to play oriented toward scoring goals and involves a constant effort to move the team's own players and the ball up the field toward the opposing team's end. The attacking team is taking a risk because in spreading its players over the whole field with many of them in the opposing team's half, it weakens the defense of its own goal. In contrast, a defensive style is oriented toward preventing the opposing team from scoring goals by closing in on itself, keeping the majority of the team's players in its own end of the field. While this style usually lessens a team's chance of scoring a goal, it can produce goals through a counter-attack, taking advantage of the defensively weak position of an attacking opposing team. Both these styles are considered to be effective strategies when used at the appropriate time in a game. If a team is losing, it should attack; if it is winning, it should play defensively. If the game is tied, a team can either combine the strategies or employ the one that it does better, so that teams may come to be known for their tendency toward one style or the other.

Porra members express distaste for the defensive style, claiming that at best it constitutes a good, but boring, rational strategy for winning games. At worst, it is really a veiled version of clientelism, as I explain further below. They boast that even if the Pumas are winning, the team continues to attack despite the risk that the opposing team might score with a counter-attack. According to the porra members, when the Pumas attack they are not simply following a rational, objective, predetermined plan for scoring goals or winning games. Rather, their attacking style is a risk-taking, unpredictable, and passionate expression of their love for the game and for the team's *camiseta* (jersey) and *colores* (colors). Héctor, a twenty-five-year-old accountant, described the Pumas' style as, "Such a harmonious form. For me, how soccer should be played: joyously, attacking, moving ahead. Not like Necaxa[3] or América that stay back and then suddenly score. I prefer a style of soccer with a lot of passing; an open game." Porra members add, moreover, that what passes as a strategic defensive style among teams in the Mexican league is, in reality, passive, indifferent, and fearful play: a manifestation of clientelistic interests that have nothing to do with winning soccer games. They describe two types of clientelistic relations to explain and conceptualize this style. One type, conceptualized through the family idiom of *el consentido* (the favorite or spoiled child), accounts for the clientelistic involvement of star players, and the other, often imagined through the idiom of the mafia (see below), accounts for the rest.

El Consentido

According to porra members, when teams other than the Pumas contract star players, a set of exchanges between team and player begins that goes beyond and even eclipses the exchange of a big salary for a high level of performance. The team publicly praises the player excessively, denying his mistakes on the field and shielding him from criticism. In exchange, the player is expected to demonstrate loyalty to the team by praising it, denying its negative aspects such as the mistreatment of other players, and expressing his desire to remain with the team. They state that the relationships between the América Football Club and its star players exemplify this type of exchange. Because the television network Televisa owns the team, the television broadcasts of the game provide a ready medium for the promotion and praise of star players. According to Héctor, "América gets good players and I would even say that they have a good team if you could ever see them without the protection of Televisa. Watching a Televisa broadcast, if an América player fouls a Pumas player, it was a good play, 'Going for the ball.' But if a Pumas player fouls an América player in the same way, it was 'a dangerous foul.'" Group members also claim that Televisa provides star players with entry into the glamorous world of the country's elite entertainers. Once within this world, the players have frequent opportunities during interviews and public appearances to praise the team and Televisa.

The porra members see this relationship as more than a simple exchange between discrete actors. They assert that it completely reorients the player's personality toward the exchange of praise, replacing any previous orientation toward either passionate or rationalized soccer play. They conceptualize this process of transformation and its result through the idiom of el consentido. They state that *el equipo consiente al jugador* (the team favors/spoils the player) through excessive praise, transforming him into someone akin to a spoiled child.

A rough sketch of the type of parent-child relationship that Mexicans evoke when they use *consentir* (to favor or to spoil) will help to clarify what the porra members are trying to get across. In describing family dynamics, almost everyone will label one or more of their siblings *el consentido de mi mamá/de mi papá* (the favorite or spoiled one of my mom/of my dad). The two most significant features of the relationship between parent and consentido are its inappropriateness and its transformative quality. The relationship is inappropriate because it replaces the exchanges defined by the accepted relationship between parents and children with exchanges driven by the particular emotional needs of the individuals involved. In other words, a parent favors a son or daughter not for their superior performance in the role of son or daughter, but because the child as a particular person fulfills for the parent an emotional need beyond the generalized parent-child relationship. The relationship is transformative in that the child learns to believe in his or her supposed superiority and to expect favoritism and praise without having performed in an appropriate manner. Moreover, the child comes to share with the parent an emotional dependence on the relationship.

As the English term "spoiled" suggests, the child's personality has been negatively oriented by the relationship in a general sense, leading him or her to expect special treatment in other contexts as well.

When the porra members describe a player as a consentido, they are referring to the fact that he is no longer concerned with exciting or effective performance as a soccer player and instead directs his efforts to the only thing he now knows: demonstrating the loyalty that the team wants in exchange for favoritism. They state that spoiled players do not bother to run for a ball if it is a few meters away because they are indifferent about the game and unwilling to endanger the quality of their next television appearance by risking injury, getting dirty, or messing up their hair. They note that all opposing teams, but especially América, attempt to recruit and spoil players with specific characteristics, unrelated to soccer, such as light skin and stylish hairdos, that could serve to forward an owner's elitist pretensions. For example, once I was watching television with Daniel when an interview with Luis García, a former Pumas player then with América, came on. Daniel expressed his belief that América had contracted and promoted García as a star because of his light skin color and European facial features. He theorized that because of the association of these physical characteristics with the rich and powerful, both at a national and a global level, a player like García helps confirm the link between América and economic ascendancy.[4]

Further, club members are quick to recognize and criticize the occasional Pumas player who attempts to signal, through praise for opposing teams and through an exaggerated concern with his physical appearance, a desire to play for another team and become a consentido. For example, they declared their anger with one Pumas player, Braulio Luna, for playing as if he cared more about his long stylish hair than about the outcome of the game and because he had stated during an interview that he was an América fan as a child. They assured me that América would soon hire him away from the Pumas. I doubted the prediction, thinking that a more soccer-based logic would determine team owners' decisions. However, América did sign Luna soon after, apparently confirming my informants' theory, although of course I have no way of knowing the real reason behind his move.

According to the porra members, there is no genuine heartfelt loyalty involved in the relationship between team and consentido, because the players are only performing loyalty for the team to obtain the praise they have come to depend upon. They declare that genuine loyalty, the loyalty based on heartfelt allegiance and not motivated by self-interest, such as the kind embodied by Pumas players, is only possible in the absence of clientelistic relations. Their conceptualization of the negative relationship between clientelism and loyalty suggests a need for caution regarding the scholarly premise that loyalty is one of the bases of the enduring bonds that constitute clientelistic relations (Roniger 1990; Lomnitz-Adler 1992; Pansters 1997). The fact that actors frequently portray clientelistic relationships in terms of loyalty does not necessarily mean that genuine feelings of loyalty can explain the existence, durability, and strength of the bond. I should note, moreover, that while porra members employ the idiom of the consentido in a particularly revealing manner, it is widely used by Mexico City residents to refer to clientelism when it involves key personalities, such as leaders of popular movements, and their co-optation.

The Mafia and Obedience

According to my informants, although only a few players on any one of the other teams are transformed into clients through consentimiento, none of them escape clientelism's pernicious influence. Teams other than the Pumas transform the players they do not consider worthy of favoritism into clients through demands of strict obedience. Porra members explain that instead of expecting exciting or effective play from these players, the teams demand, first and foremost, absolute acquiescence to the management's wishes. An exchange of employment for obedience substitutes for the exchange of a salary for soccer play, making the reproduction of hierarchy and authority an end in itself. Once more, the club members claim that this is not simply an isolated exchange between discrete individuals. Rather, this constant emphasis on obedience transforms the personality of the player, orienting him toward a single objective: compliance to avoid sanctions and to keep his job. As in the case of the consentidos, they insist that this obedience should not be confused with authentic loyalty because it is inspired by fear and not by genuine heartfelt allegiance.

Porra members frequently use the metaphor of the mafia to describe this pervasive atmosphere of obedience inspired by fear of punishment and loss. Juan, a twenty-year-old fan who works for the city's subway system and hopes to study at the UNAM, described the situation this way, "The soccer here in Mexico is very corrupt. The leaders of the federation, of the teams, are very corrupt. It has become a sort of mafia and the Pumas have always been characterized by the fact that they do not enter into that game of the mafia. I like that for the most part the [Pumas] team has young players. I'm young and you could say that at my age I could even be playing with the team. . . . I like how they play, how they move the game forward and push the play up the field." It is important to distinguish between what Mexico City residents mean when they call something *una mafia* and common notions of the mafia in the English-speaking world derived from movies such as "The Godfather." When the term is used in the former context, it calls up suspicions of a hierarchical pyramid-shaped organization in which permission to run a small "independent" business along with a bit of protection flows downward while part of the profits and obedience flow upward. Those at the top of the pyramid use coercion and sometimes violence to control those below them, and, in addition, those on top will organize those on bottom as a violent force against threats to the whole organization. I use the term "suspicions" because only the base, in the form of a series of apparently independent actors or small businesses, is visible to external observers. The

invisible organization of the privately owned buses that constitute the public transport system in parts of Mexico City and
the hidden organization of different types of street vendors are
examples of what people frequently refer to as una mafia. While
kinship and *padrinazgo* (godparenthood) relationships may be
involved, they are not considered to be of primary importance,
as is the case of the mafia usually depicted in movies.

As I stated above, the porra members, like other Mexico
City residents, imagine an urban clientelism, which because
of its sheer size, depends less on loyalties based on traditional,
personalized relationships and more on relatively impersonal
relationships tightly controlled through coercion and violence.
Although not kinship-based in nature, this tight control extends
to clients' families, sometimes because the whole family participates in the organization's activities, and always as the potential
target for a threat to keep clients in line. Thus, when the porra
members refer to soccer-related organizations as a mafia, they
suggest two things. First, they suggest that Mexican soccer is not
what it appears to be: a screen of contractual market exchanges
veils a social order of hierarchy, authoritarianism, and coercion
aimed at its own reproduction and at illicitly extracting a profit
from those on bottom. Second, they propose that the corruption of Mexican soccer is not restricted to isolated exchanges
between bounded individuals in a workplace, but rather constitutes a whole way of life, as the coercion, obedience, and fear
extend into people's homes and minds.

Porra members contend that this whole way of life manifests on the soccer field as passive and predictable play. They
explain that even if teams demand effective and exciting play
and players obediently attempt to comply, because good soccer requires creativity, spontaneity, and risk-taking, the players
inevitably fail. Focused as they are on obedience and not on the
game itself, their attempts to play well are no more than imi-
tations or performances of good soccer and thus are eminently
predictable. Further, because they fear that a failed risk could
be interpreted as disobedience, their play is conservative and

passive in the extreme. Thus, according to the club members, while the consentidos approach soccer play with an attitude of indifference and the rest of the players approach it fearing the consequences of disobedience, the two orientations combine to produce one overall effect: predictable and passive soccer, lacking both the strategic capacity of a defensive style and, more importantly, an attacking style's potential for excitement. Or, as one porra member said of the uninspired play of opposing players, "You can buy a player's legs, but not his heart."

According to the porra members, the Pumas team is different for two interconnected reasons: its unique not-for-profit organization and the youth of its players. They suggest that the team's unique form of ownership allows it to escape domination by the capitalist market and its logic. As proof of this escape, they often point out that the Pumas is the only professional team in Mexico without advertisements on its uniforms. They claim that because the team management is not blinded by capitalist logic, it appreciates the importance of other aspects of soccer besides winning, such as creativity and risk-taking. Therefore, even though seemingly a questionable approach to winning championships against teams with more experienced, mature players, the team continues to contract the unproven young players whom no other team is willing to take a chance on, but whose creativity and spontaneity has not yet been stifled by the discipline of strategic rationalization.

The porra members add, moreover, that the philosophy of puros jóvenes is especially significant in the Mexican context of pervasive clientelism. Not only are young players undisciplined, in addition, employers have not yet transformed them into consentidos or fearful clients. The players have not been around long enough to become famous and so no team is interested in favoring and spoiling them. Meanwhile, because previous employers have not yet oriented their personalities toward fear-inspired compliance and because they have no dependents, other teams see them as potentially too volatile to be obedient clients. The Pumas team, in contrast, *dándoles chance a los jóvenes* (giving young players a chance), ends up with players who are free from the stifling effects of rationalization and of clientelism. Because their play is inspired by genuine heartfelt love for the game rather than the external and confining influences of rationalism or clientelism, it is spontaneous, creative, and joyful. Furthermore, although the group members state that victories and championships are not the main objective of the puros jóvenes philosophy, they relate the team's success to it. Accordingly, because the other teams in the Mexican league are dominated by clientelistic relations, the Pumas win games and championships despite their risk-taking style of play and lack of experience.

The Ideal versus Reality

The porra members' representations of the Pumas' and the opposing teams' styles of play should not be mistaken for descriptions of what actually happens on the field. If the Pumas never played a defensive style and if the other teams never attacked, it is unlikely any of them would last very long in the league's first division.[5] Undoubtedly, some teams tend toward a more attack-oriented or a more defensive style, although this tendency may vary with changes in coaches and players. Furthermore, most teams in the league do field some young players, and a few have established their own fuerzas básicas. Meanwhile, the Pumas usually fields one or two older players. These are generally players who started with the Pumas and then went to another team before returning. Porra members explained that these players add an element of experience to the team and teach the younger players, while understanding the Pumas' philosophy. Despite these variations in playing style and team makeup from the team's philosophy, even beyond its fans the Pumas is known to play an attack-oriented style and to field younger players compared to other teams in the league, and my untrained soccer eye suggests that this reputation is deserved. Yet, while this reputation and its "objective" basis are significant because they make the Pumas a viable object for the porra members' representations, they are not the essence of their understanding of the relationship between their claims and actual soccer play.

The porra members are not simply biased observers of their favorite team. Rather, they readily admit that the Pumas team and players play defensively and even passively at times. Such admissions are not contradictions, because in their claims they are referring to something that takes form in actual events and actions but that exists independently of them. According to group members, *ser Puma* (to be Puma) is not reducible to the performances or actions of players, coaches, and managers. Rather, ser Puma is to put into practice the universal human potential to live life as an expression of our innermost, heartfelt desires. These heartfelt desires are embodied in particular Pumas players, in moments during a game, during specific games, and across certain whole seasons. At times, porra members claim that certain players or the whole team is straying from the Pumas ideal. At these moments, they see themselves as the ideal's principal upholders among the Pumas' fans, players, and management. Divergence from this ideal by the Pumas team or its players disappoints or angers them, but it does not come as a surprise because it only proves their point that clientelism is pervasive in Mexican society.

The porra members realize that even their favorite, most passionate young players cannot embody the ideal permanently. They expect that young players will leave the team when other teams offer them more money. They note that some of those players wholeheartedly adopt the clientelistic relations and passive play of other teams and thus become objects of their scorn, whereas others who do their best to maintain a bit of the Pumas ideal in hostile circumstances win their admiration. The lack of this latter type of ex-Pumas players in no way threatens the Pumas ideal, which is independent of actual performances of Pumas players, former or present. This type of former Pumas player does, however, give the club members hope that the confusion of means with ends can be straightened out, that is, that passionate players can be compensated with higher pay without becoming clients.

They are also aware that most Pumas players are drastically underpaid compared to other players in the league and thus even they are not compensated for their passionate play. The porra members are not ascetics, and they believe that the Pumas players deserve higher salaries. They usually place blame for this discrepancy not on the Pumas management itself but on the manner in which other teams' clientelistic logic closes young players out of the market. However, when the management sold or traded one of their favorite players to another team, supposedly because their value had grown too great for the team's low budget, I heard group members voice suspicions about the honesty of the team's not-for-profit management, wondering why the earnings from television contracts and ticket sales do not leave more money for the players. I do not have data on the Pumas' earnings and spending, so I cannot comment on whether the management exploits young players' disadvantage in the market for profit or whether the team exists "to give young players a chance" and does not profit from them beyond fulfilling the team's financial necessities. I must reiterate, however, that the porra members do not see the possibility of corruption within the Pumas organization as a threat to the ideal of ser Puma. Rather, they see it as proof of the pervasiveness of clientelism and of the need for a stance against it.

Contrasting Cheering Styles

Porra members not only recognize the stifling effects of clientelistic relationships and scientific objectivity or democratic rationality on styles of soccer play, they also claim that these relationships have an effect on fans' cheering. They conceptualize their own cheering in a manner similar to the way they describe the Pumas' style of play. Because they are free from the oppressive effects of clientelism and the dulling effects of objectivity and rationality, their cheering originates in their hearts, inspired by a love for the game and the team, and thus it is spontaneous, passionate, and creative. In contrast, opposing fans' cheering is, according to my informants, an attempt to please their team and not a spontaneous expression of heartfelt love for it. Porra members explain that opposing fans cheer to please their team because their jobs have transformed them into fearful, obedient, eager-to-please clients who no longer know how to act in any other manner. They claim that their own cheering is distinct because as youths, excluded from the job market, they have not yet been turned into clients.

Obtaining Porra Membership

A conflict between the porra members and Ernesto regarding the criteria for admitting new members to the group is illustrative of the contrast the young fans draw between their own cheering versus action guided by the external influences of clientelism or democratic rationality. Just months before I began my research, the porra was still unofficially, but indisputably led by Javier, a charismatic man in his late thirties. Porra members remembered him as a sort of benevolent dictator who made all the decisions for the group including which cheers they would recite during games. They stated that no one even thought to question his leadership. When Javier left the group, Ernesto became the porra's first president. Drawing on the wave of democratic rhetoric sweeping the country, he called for an election to choose a president for the group and for meetings to reach decisions collectively. Ernesto himself won the election. While porra members latter admitted that Ernesto's democratic leadership made possible the critical perspective they never thought to develop under Javier, they soon directed their criticism toward Ernesto, his democratic rationality, and the corruption they claimed that his democracy served to obscure. Ernesto stated that during Javier's time, decisions about including new members were personalized and arbitrary, as Javier admitted those he liked and excluded those he did not. Thus, Ernesto set about establishing a set of objective rules for membership. He proposed that new members would be admitted when they could demonstrate that they had attended a minimum number of consecutive games and that they knew all of the cheers. He asked the current members for photos and printed up identification cards, so that only those with a card would receive the benefits of membership: permission to sit in the porra's roped off area of the stands and free or discounted tickets for games.

Porra members noted, however, that Ernesto used his supposedly objective criteria to legitimate his personal decisions to admit new members in exchange for their loyalty. Although they expressed disgust at his clientelistic practices, they also laughed at his attempts to rationalize membership, using it as evidence that he, no longer a youth, had forgotten the true meaning of Pumas fandom. They explained that, for them, new membership is a process of mutual attraction between the group and the potential member. A potential member is drawn to the porra's section by his heartfelt affinity for the club's passionate cheering, just as previously he was drawn to the team and the stadium. After sitting on the margins of the porra's section for a few games, the porra members are drawn to the fan's passionate cheering and invite him to sit in the section. Thus, emotive expression and heartfelt affinity determine membership, not simply attendance or knowing cheers. A fan who asks what he has to do to join is an inappropriate member because he does not understand that passionate cheering leads to membership and not the other way around. The criteria for membership are meant to be sensed, not measured, and being a Pumas fan is not something one chooses as if he were a consumer, but rather something one feels.

Supporting the Team

Porra members assert that because their cheering originates within them and extends outward to the team, it has the potential to inspire the players and thus affect the outcome of the game.

At first, when they insisted to me that they go to the stadium *para apoyar* (to support) the team, I ignored it as a statement of the obvious: all fans go to the stadium to support their team. However, I later learned that group members believe that most fans in Mexico do not go to the stadium to support their team, but rather to demonstrate their obedience to it. While porra members describe their own cheering as supportive and active and thus with the potential to produce inspired play, goals, and victories, they state that opposing fans cheer in a reactive or passive manner. They explain that opposing fans only cheer after their team scores a goal and that this cheering is a performance of the inauthentic loyalty of the client rather than a heartfelt celebration. The following extraction from my field notes exemplifies their efforts to make this distinction:

> Hanging around outside of the CU stadium before a game against América, watching large numbers of flag-carrying América fans enter, Jorge commented that the América fans would be quiet because they only cheer after a goal. At the time I was not sure what he meant, but it turned out to be more or less the case as I observed the game. The América fans completely filled the opposite half of the 70,000-seat stadium, but they did not make much noise during the game. They waved their flags and cheered when América came onto the field and when the team scored. They also yelled "goooool" [goal] during corner kicks, but otherwise they sat and were quiet. Meanwhile the Pumas' side of the stadium boomed with cheers led by the porra throughout the game.

Creative Expression through Songs

The porra members also interpret the differences between the content and form of their own cheers and those of opposing fans in terms of the internally inspired versus obedience and the active versus passive distinctions. They note that the fans of all the other teams, if they cheer in unison at all, generally use the same cheer, the Chíquiti Bom, to celebrate their team's goals:

Chíquiti bom a la bim bom bam
Chíquiti bom a la bim bom bam
A la bio, a la bao,
A la bim bom bam
[team name], [team name]
¡Ra ra ra!

Rafael, a twenty-one-year-old political science student at the UNAM, explained to me that the Chíquiti Bom is *una porra* (a cheer, hence the name given to the fan clubs), but that most of the porra members prefer *cantos* (songs) to porras. He explained that *se canta* (one sings) a song whereas *se grita* (one shouts) a porra, and because it is impossible to shout during the whole game, it is necessary to sit down and rest after each porra. However, it is possible to stand and sing songs throughout the whole game and thereby express love for and support the team in a more constant manner. Porra members add that songs offer greater opportunity for nonverbal expression of their love for the team. They can more easily jump up and down, sway from side to side, or wave their arms while singing than while shouting.

Furthermore, according to porra members, whereas the Chíquiti Bom contains no words of inspiration, their cantos actively support and inspire the players and other fans by creatively expressing their love for the team. Here are the lyrics of three of their cantos:

Sí, sí señores yo soy de Pumas	Yes, yes sir I am of the Pumas
Sí, sí señores de corazón	Yes, yes sir from the heart
Sí, sí señores quiero que sea	Yes, yes sir I want them to be
Que sea Pumas	I want Pumas to be
Por Dios nuevo campeón	By God the new champion
Vamos Pumas, vamos Pumas	Let's go Pumas, let's go Pumas
Vamos Pumas, vamos a ganar	Let's go Pumas, we're going to win

Qué esta porra siempre	This porra will always
te va a apoyar, ¡Pumas!	support you, Pumas!
Por la gloria, por la gloria	For the glory, for the glory
de la UNAM	of the UNAM
De la UNAM, de la UNAM	Of the UNAM, of the UNAM
Pan y vino, pan y vino	Bread and wine, bread and wine
Pan y vino, pan y vino	Bread and wine, bread and wine
Él que no grite por Pumas	If you aren't shouting for the Pumas
¿Para qué chingados vino?	Why the hell did you come?

Note that all three songs refer not just to the Pumas, but to the porra as well, emphasizing their love for and support of the team. The last of these songs is directed at group members or Pumas fans who are not cheering or who are not cheering with passion.

Finally, porra members distinguish between the creativity involved in their constant invention of new songs and the conformist manner in which opposing fans always shout the same generic cheer, the Chíquiti Bom. They claim that their genuine love for the team manifests itself even between games in the active and creative process of inventing new songs by putting their own lyrics to the catchy tunes of popular songs or by adapting Argentine and Chilean fans' songs that they hear on television.

As with the porra members' claims about playing styles, their statements about cheering contribute to a subaltern conceptualization of clientelism and of an alternative other than modern democracy, but they should not be mistaken for a reliable interpretation of the practices of opposing fans or for a comprehensive ethnography of the club members and their practices. Garry Robson's recent study of fandom among supporters of Southeast London's Millwall Football Club suggests, for example, a very different interpretation of the Chíquiti Bom's lack of explicitly supportive lyrics. Robson sees fans' wordless cheers as exemplary of their resolutely nonbourgeois, nondiscursive, but rather bodily and practical working-class habitus (2000:170,

183). It would not surprise me if an ethnographic study of working-class Mexican fans reached a similar conclusion. In fact, I would not expect those of the porra, with their own middle-class backgrounds or aspirations, to be particularly appreciative of such working-class forms of expression. Their critique, rather, displays a bourgeois affinity for the discursive, although it by no means lacks a nonverbal component.

Clientelism within the Porra

As we will see in the following chapters, some of the very upholders of this anticlientelistic stance do not escape clientelism and its effects. Ernesto, the club's president, cultivates clientelistic relations among members to secure their loyalty and obedience, thereby assuring the continuation of his leadership position and of his own clientelistic relationship with the team management. He attempts to spoil the charismatic, informal leaders among the young members, offering them flattery, a share of his power, and extra tickets for their close friends. Some of the porra members who are not informal leaders approach Ernesto or his consentidos in the style of fearful clients, offering up their obedience in exchange for an assurance of receiving full membership privileges. As I mentioned above, there is not always a clear division between those who enter clientelistic relations and those who resist them, so that a club member who complains about corruption one moment could be seen falling for Ernesto's attempts, through flattery and gift-giving, to spoil him the next.

Despite, or perhaps precisely because of this constant danger to all, the acceptance of or attempt to initiate such relations with Ernesto always provokes criticism among fellow porra members. Often, they express this criticism in an idiom more denigrating than that of el consentido, referring to the porra member as Ernesto's *picador* (the bullfighter who goads the bull by pricking it with a rod). The use of this label evokes a culturally specific homosexual relationship between an older and wealthy gay man and a "straight" young man in which the latter exchanges sex for privileges and gifts. This portrayal insults Ernesto by making him out to be *un puto* (a man who likes to be penetrated sexually by other men), but the statement is really directed at the porra member. Although the client's masculinity is not called into question because he is portrayed as a penetrator, an unambiguously masculine sexual role in many Latin American contexts (see Lancaster 1988), this sexual role is undoubtedly stigmatized as aberrant and shameful according to most men in Mexico City (see Prieur 1998:188). In contrast to the consentido, who can be forgiven because of his status as a childlike victim, albeit a complacent one, the picador is made to feel ashamed of his willing participation in the relationship. Porra members' teasing or insulting of Ernesto's clients makes for some fun at their expense but also discourages them and any potential clients who are listening from participating in such relationships. Thus, the porra members' denigrating portrayals of clientelism help to uphold the Pumas fans' social project among the group's members themselves.

In the next chapter I describe how a struggle between the president and his clients versus the members resisting his clientelism plays out in a struggle over cheering styles in the stadium during games. The president attempts to impose centrally organized cheering in which one of his consentidos stands in front of the group and leads the cheers. Ernesto tells the consentido which cheers to lead, generally favoring well-known, established porras (shouted cheers) over recently composed songs. Meanwhile, his opposition breaks spontaneously into songs with no apparent leader, interrupting Ernesto's centralized organization. This battle over the verbal territory of the porra is really a conflict over what kinds of social relations and actions should constitute the club: the president's clientelism disguised as democratic rationalism or the young members' ideal of authentic heartfelt expression.

This conflict reminds us that, even within the group, some members participate in clientelistic relations, while continuing to claim an anticlientelistic stance. Furthermore, the fact that some members—usually from the eastern part of the city—approach Ernesto as clients suggests that they already have experience with such relations in other contexts such as the workplace.[6] Despite this undeniable participation of certain porra members in clientelistic relations, it is important to note that they do not perceive this inconsistency as a threat to their anticlientelistic stance because they locate the essence of the ideal of ser Puma in the universal human potential for heartfelt expression and not in what actors do on the field or in the stands. Furthermore, they consider the presence of clientelism within the group as proof of the pervasiveness of the problem in Mexico and of the need for a stance against it.

Political and Economic Transition, Romanticism, and the Pumas Project

An anthropological treatment of this ideal vision for Mexican society is incomplete without an attempt to place it within the wider cultural and historical context from which it emerges. Although I sometimes borrow ideas from the porra members, adopting their concerns as my own, this is one point at which I do not wish to do so. That is, I am uncomfortable with the idea that the porra members' vision is truly a reflection of the basically and universally human. Instead, I suspect that it is a reflection of a culturally and historically particular manner of seeing the world, which includes certain assumptions about what is universally human.

Their ideal vision first struck me, and perhaps other readers familiar with the anthropological literature as well, as similar to what Victor Turner (1969) called "communitas." Turner studied and wrote about the African people known as the Ndembu in the 1950s and 1960s, a time when British social anthropology was dominated by an interest in social structure. Turner's interest in rituals, however, led him to observe moments in Ndembu social life when the overall structure of society was downplayed. Consequently, he suggested that social life is a process of oscillation between structure and moments of antistructure and that the latter result in the renewal or even the transformation of the former. Turner then formulated the concept of communitas to describe the mode of sociality he believed to have observed during moments of antistructure: stripped of their roles in political, legal, and economic hierarchies, actors meet and find comradeship in the lowest common denominator, their humanness (1969:96–97). According to Turner, in the absence of structure's demands, action during moments of communitas is spontaneous and can also be critical and creative. He also makes reference to actors' innocence and purity in moments of communitas due to their return to a natural human state (1969:136). The equation between communitas and porra members' ideal of spontaneous, authentic, heartfelt action as opposed to the hierarchy of clientelism or the objective conventions of modern democracy and science requires no elaboration. The usefulness of Turner's formulation in my analysis reaches its limits, however, in that he simply repeats the porra members' explanation that their vision has its origins in the basically and universally human.

It is notable that Turner's Western examples of communitas—from the philosophy of Martin Buber to the hippie movement—conform to his universal formulation quite well, whereas his African examples generally do not. As another Africanist, T. O. Beidelman (1980), has noted, most of Turner's examples of communitas in African societies reveal an emphasis upon or an exaggeration of one aspect of social structure rather than a total absence of structure. Ironically, Turner mentioned that he was criticized for applying the concept, first formulated in his work on preliterate Africa, to modern society (1969: vi). In contrast, I would say that it is in relation to modern society that the concept is most relevant, but as a description of a culturally specific phenomenon and not as a universally applicable analytical concept. Thus, as even Turner himself recognized at one point (1969:126), Rousseau, Shakespeare's characters, and the philosopher Martin Buber should be treated as native informants rather than fellow theorists.

This reflection on Turner's communitas suggested that my search for the context from which the porra members' ideal vision emerges had to extend beyond Mexico to the modern West more generally. My search ended coincidentally, when I came across an article by political scientist Yvon Grenier, "The Romantic Liberalism of Octavio Paz" (2001b). The similarities between Grenier's description of the Romantic critique that inspired Mexican poet and essayist Octavio Paz and the porra members' critical vision of Mexican society struck me immediately. Perhaps this connection is no great revelation to readers familiar with the Romantic movement, but I imagine that I am not the first student of contemporary Mexican popular culture to omit the history of European art and poetry from my list of relevant literature.

Further exploration of the history of Romanticism confirmed my initial impression of similarity and suggested that both critical visions emerged under similar circumstances. The historian J. L. Talmon interpreted Romanticism "as the sum total of the ways in which man's self-awareness was affected by the Revolutionary-Napoleonic disruption, and in which he tried to take his bearings in a world that had lost its 'fixities' and 'definities'" (1967:136). Talmon also noted that revolutionary expectations "far outran the realities of objective change" (1967:12). Thus, in the political sphere, the Romantic was concerned with the "restrictions imposed by religious tradition, political absolutism and a hierarchical social system in order to express and determine himself and create the kind of order in which he wished to live" (1967:136). Likewise, porra members have developed their ideal vision of society, which favors free individual expression over all externally imposed order, in the context of the breaking down of Mexico's hierarchical clientelistic social structure.

The Romantic Movement was also a critique of and uprising against tradition's enemy, rationalism. According to Talmon, "the Romantic craved not to find the same universal truth, but to experience reality in a way wholly his own. This was not to be done by reasoning, but through feeling, sentiment, imagination, instinct, passion, dream and recollection" (1967:139). Grenier reflected the Romantic's impassioned form of expression when he refers to art's claim to wake the nonart world from its "rationalist nightmare" (2001a:57) by opposing "heart" to "reason" (2001a:55). Similarly, the porra members are quick to reject clientelism's standard replacement, democracy, as seen in their reaction to Ernesto's attempts to rationalize porra membership and their cheering, and to insist instead on action driven by heartfelt emotion. Another parallel is between art's claim to guide the nonart world and the young porra members' alleged guidance of people of all ages: artists and youth hold privileged positions beyond the influence of externally imposed orders, but each uses this privilege not to exclude others but to lead them out of darkness. Art and youthfulness are means to ends and not isolated subcultures.

Grenier also adds subtlety to our understanding of the relationship between Romanticism and rationalism: "Romanticism is not so much the opposite of the Enlightenment as its shadow" (2001a:56). That is, its emergence is unimaginable without the freedom from tradition and the promotion of self-criticism that are central to Enlightenment and modernity (2001a:80). Romanticism thus accepts rationalism and democracy as means to an end but reject them as ends in themselves, as when progress is narrowly defined to mean modernization. Similarly, I have suggested that the porra members recognize that their critical vision flourished only after Ernesto rejected the previous president's authoritarian practices in favor of a democratic organization. They are not antidemocratic, but they argue that their objective is not the democratization of the porra, but rather the creation of conditions necessary for passionate support of the team.

This distinction between the porra members' ideal vision and democracy is most clearly illustrated in the disagreement between Ernesto and the young porra members over how to determine porra membership. While Ernesto tried to establish something like citizenship with objectively measurable criteria, the young porra members claimed that membership could only be determined by a fan's passion for the team, which could only be felt and not measured. Along similar lines, the Pumas fans' ideal vision is not so much the opposite of liberalism as its shadow, to adopt Grenier's phrase. Their ideal vision mirrors or perhaps even adopts aspects of liberalism, with its emphasis on self-government, in the sense that it looks inward for guidance. However, the fans also reject the notion of free choice that usually accompanies self-government in this ideal liberal individual and consumer, instead saying that being a Pumas fan is something that one feels rather than chooses.

Unlike Turner's communitas, Romanticism can be contextualized within a particular historical moment; thus, the comparison has helped me to situate the porra members' critical vision within a broader social context. In a manner analogous to Romanticism, their critical vision has been made possible by, but is also a reaction to, the incomplete breakdown of Mexico's pyramidical clientelistic social structure in the context of neoliberal budgetary cuts and the democratic discourse and organization that filled many of the gaps left by the old structure. By drawing this comparison with the eighteenth- and nineteenth-century European movement, I am not simply attempting to categorize the porra members' vision, nor do I believe these similarities between Pumas fandom and literary Romanticism are due to the former's imitation of the latter. Rather, I suggest that they are independent reactions to parallel circumstances.

In the following chapter, I provide an ethnographic account of how the porra members put their ideal vision for society into action during a typical game day, in and around the stadium. A conflict between the young porra members and the group's president over the group's social form emerges as a clash between cheering styles. I also introduce data on masculinity, as porra members try to distinguish and distance themselves from female fans and from their own interests in romantic and domestic relationships.

3

A Day at the Stadium

The Clash of Cheering Styles and Modes of Sociality

My objective in this chapter is to provide an ethnographic portrayal of how the porra members put their ideal vision for society into action. I do so by describing their practices during a typical game day, in and around the stadium. Putting their ideal vision into action, however, is not a straightforward process. Rather, it involves a near constant effort on the part of the club members to mark off their preferred manner of being as distinct from all others. I discuss how they attempt to mark it off from the variety of modes of sociality that exist outside the stadium in other contexts such as the family, work, and school, as well as from internal threats including Ernesto's clientelism and what the male members imagine as the female porra members' sexuality and domesticity. Thus, the porra members are not simply living their ideal vision, they are actively creating it. This creation, coupled with resistance to the influence of other modes of sociality, could be referred to as the "Puma-ization" or, in more general terms, the "romanticization" of the time and space involved.

As I suggested at the end of the previous chapter, this process of Puma-ization or romanticization could be likened to the creation of what Victor Turner referred to as communitas, in that the porra members themselves imagine their ideal mode of sociality as a sort of antistructure. They claim that as youths they continue to exist in what might be termed a presocialized state, in the sense that they have not yet been fitted into the roles and relationships that constitute the structure of society. It is precisely because of this presocialized state that porra members are free to express their individual emotions in a manner that people whose actions are guided by others or by objective rational cannot. I refer here to socialization in this specific sense of "roles" and "structures," because porra members in no way wish to be generally antisocial. Rather, they state the importance of sharing individually generated emotions and expressing them collectively with others who feel the same way. According to porra members, this desire is part of what draws them to the stadium each week. Thus, their ideal mode of sociality is one without the external limitations placed on individual action by roles and structures. Instead, a meeting of individuals as persons, and nothing more or less, provides an ideal atmosphere for the free expression of heartfelt emotion.

"Are You Ready for el Desmadre?": Gathering Outside the Stadium Before a Game

For the porra members, game-day activities begin in the parking lot outside of the stadium three hours before the game begins. Home games are usually played every other week on Sundays at noon, but sometimes they are scheduled later in the day or on another day of the week. The stadium, built in the 1950s as part of the new University City, is meant to recall a pre-Columbian indigenous pyramid. Walls of roughly cut stone curve upward from the ground, concealing the stadium's concrete and steel structure. A mural in relief, designed by the Mexican artist Diego Rivera, graces the center of one wall. Entitled "The University, the Family, and Sport in Mexico," the mural features the university crest, Mexican national imagery with its prominent prehispanic themes, and more universal imagery including the family, the peace dove, and the Olympic flame. The mural connects the stadium to the modernist academic buildings, just across Insurgentes Avenue, which are adorned with other Diego Rivera murals featuring various nationalist and pan–Latin American themes including more references to prehispanic civilization.

Most of the porra members travel to the stadium by public transportation, coming from all parts of the metropolis. For many, this means an hour or two of travel to the stadium, taking one bus to the subway, the subway to the stop nearest the stadium, and then another short bus ride the rest of the way.[1] Porra members must get to the stadium early to make sure they receive a free or subsidized ticket (see below). However, porra members do not just arrive early out of necessity. They come to spend time with others who share the same ideal vision and the same preference for a particular way of being, but whom they do not have any other opportunity to see because of work and school schedules, long distances to travel, and a lack of a place to gather because most members live with their families.[2]

A member arriving at the edge of the stadium's parking lot sees a few groups of four or five members standing around and talking. As he approaches one of these groups, the conversation stops and the new arrival greets and is greeted by all present, giving and receiving a solid handshake from each member. The handshake is common to young men throughout Mexico City, and it begins with both members raising their right hands to the height of their shoulders before swinging them down and around to meet with a loud smack and then sliding into position for the actual shake. The harder they slap together their hands, the greater the feelings of warmth and camaraderie. Often spoken greetings are mumbled without much enthusiasm, but a more outgoing member greeting a favored friend is likely to aim a wide smile at the new arrival and exclaim, ¡¿*Qué pasó, güey*?! (What's up, man?!) or ¡¿*Estás listo para el desmadre*?! (Are you ready for the motherlessness?!).

Obviously, a term that translates literally as "motherlessness" begs for explanation. For the moment, it will suffice to say that el desmadre here refers to the playful inversion of social norms. Another term, "el cotorreo," is used interchangeably with el desmadre in this context. *Un cotorro* is a parrot and el cotorreo refers literally to the parrot's meaningless chatter, in this case extended to the young men's playful and inverting talk.

Through their opposition to social norms, these terms overlap with the porra members' critical ideal vision. However, there are also significant differences: first, the porra members' ideal vision is an alternative and not simply an inversion, and second, they take this alternative quite seriously. To understand why they use these terms metonymically to refer not just to their playfulness but to all their practices, including their impassioned support for the team, we must consider the contradiction inherent in their efforts to *impose* individual freedom of expression as part of the process of Puma-ization of the stadium's space and time. I suggest that they mediate this contradiction by not taking themselves too seriously as they do their imposing. The question, "Are you ready for el desmadre?" serves to remind the new arrival of his pending transition from usual modes of sociality to that of the porra, but without the demanding directness of saying, "Are you ready to passionately support the team?"

Thus, the greetings are not just a formality. They are a means of expressing happiness and excitement over seeing each other and the anticipation of sharing their passionate support for the team. Moreover, the greetings mark the beginning of a transition that is supposed to be complete by the time they enter the stadium. Before the first game of the season, the greetings are even more animated, both because the porra members are excited to see each other after the month-long break and because the need to mark off the time and space is particularly acute: ¡*Ahora empieza el desmadre otra vez*! (Now el desmadre is starting again!).

Over the next couple of hours, the porra member makes his way around from group to group, greeting and talking with the other members, as the groups themselves continuously grow and then dissolve. On occasion, a member feeling particularly *desmadroso* (disorderly, playful) and enterprising goes from group to group taking up a collection, referred to as *la cooperacha* (a contribution or cooperation), to buy a bottle of liquor or some beer to be passed around and finished off before the game. The collector does not ask for specific amounts and appears indiffer-

ent to the amount given or even to whether or not a contribution
is made at all. If someone does not give anything, no one will
stop him from consuming the alcohol. However, those who are
known to have money but who regularly consume more than
they contribute do gain a reputation for cheapness. Even when
no one makes a collection, a few members can be found sipping
on a spiked coke or passing around *una caguama* (a liter bottle
of beer).

Meanwhile, the porra members talk about the Pumas'
chances of making the playoffs; the team's starting line-up; the
differences in the two television stations' coverage of an international sporting event; a member's idea of inviting other porra
members to play a friendly game against his recreational soccer
team; or the pros and cons of someone's new, authentic Nike
Pumas jersey. In these discussions, porra members express earnest opinions on topics of real significance to them. They never
get very far on any topic, however, before being interrupted by
someone else's arrival and a round of greetings. Or the conversation may be broken up by a joke or *un albur* (a sexual double
entendre) aimed at someone leaving himself vulnerable by saying the wrong thing and setting himself up or by taking himself
too seriously. Once again, I understand these jokes as a manner of effecting the transition from other modes of sociality to
that of the porra, while mediating the contradiction inherent in
the collective imposition of individual freedom of expression.
For example, a fan who is just a little too earnest in his excitement over a particular player's performance is suspect of a sort
of clientelistic attitude toward the player in which his support
is guided or misguided by an effort to please an idol. Instead
of spelling all of this out, other members will discipline him by
playfully insinuating a homosexual relationship between him
and the player, by asking, ¿*Te gusta*? (Do you like him?). The
insinuation undoubtedly reinforces the stigmatization of homosexuality, but in an immediate sense it extends the stigmatization
that already exists to clientelistic relations. While porra members attempt to influence and discipline through such teasing,

more direct authoritarian attempts to discipline usual fail. For example, when a porra member demands authoritatively that others support the team and stop fooling around, they usually react by ignoring him and stepping up their desmadre. Or they may confront him more directly, but still in a joking manner, by comparing him to Ernesto, with a sarcastic response such as *Sí, Lic* (Yes, Lawyer).

Before a playoff game or a game against one of the other national teams, the porra members speak more loudly, make more jokes, and drink more due to their increased excitement and anxiety. The increased tension and the presence of large numbers of rival fans approaching the stadium also elicit playful, but heartfelt aggression from porra members.[3] A rival fan passing nearby wearing a yellow and light blue América jersey draws cries of *¡Pinche ridículo!* (Goddamn fool!) or a comment such as *Me dan asco estos colores* (Those colors make me nauseous). Porra members say these things to rival fans with a threatening look on their faces that quickly changes to a sort of devilish smile when they turn back to the group. One of the more fearless porra members, further inspired by the playful atmosphere, might run up to a fan and seize their flag or rip off their jersey and take it back to his cheering companions, as what is referred to ironically as *un recuerdo* (a souvenir). On the rare occasion when I saw a victim try to resist one of these attacks, a bunch of porra members quickly surrounded him and the victim complied immediately. Porra members claim that these verbal and physical assaults are spontaneous and bodily reactions (e.g., nausea) drawn out by rivals and their teams. However, the devilish smile or the irony in a reference to more serious violence is no less significant than the authenticity of the attacks. Once more, these verbal and physical assaults on rival fans are part of a serious but playful transition, a buildup, to the pure and unfettered support for the team and the desmadre that should exist in the stadium.

The four or five young women who attend all of the games, but who do not come with a boyfriend, husband, or brother, usually form their own group in the parking lot. They greet and are greeted by many of the young men with a mutual formality. In other words, the women and the men do not express the same excitement about seeing each other and about their common participation in the upcoming game as do the young men when they greet each other. However, the young women express happiness and excitement as they greet the other women and some of the young men. Below, I analyze further these frictions between some of the young men and the young women in the porra and the young women's resulting marginalization, but here I note the difference between young women's pregame activities compared to those of the young men.

The female porra members discuss the upcoming game not in terms of strategy and of players' abilities, but in terms of how the individual players are feeling mentally and physically. They formulate their opinions based on interviews with players in the media and on their own conversations with players during autograph sessions after games and practices. Alongside this more serious talk about the day's game, the young women discuss which players they are attracted to or which players they like and dislike personally. Again, these feelings are based on media interviews and their interactions with players in autograph sessions, but also on their observations of the players' performance on the field. Like the young men, the women say that they are Pumas fans because as youths they can relate to the young players. However, when they say this they are referring not just to a set of common experiences, such as their exclusion from work and politics, but to the possibility of creating real or imaginary platonic or romantic relationships with the players. Favorite players are those who are seen as offering the promise of such relationships, even while such promises rarely or perhaps never actually materialize. There is always recognition of the fantastic and thus playful nature of these speculations, although on some level they are serious. However, it is precisely this playfulness that the male porra members overlook or miss when they perceive the women as a threat, as I will discuss further below.

Early in his drifting from group to group, greeting, and cotor-reando, the male porra member makes his way over to el Licen-ciado Ernesto, who holds the list for tickets. The member greets the group's president with a handshake and then asks to be added to the list. The team management provides the porra with a hun-dred free tickets to every home game, giving them to Ernesto for distribution to the rest of the group. Ernesto's method of ticket distribution consists of listing all of the porra members present in order of arrival. About an hour before kickoff, he announces that he is going to begin the distribution, and the porra members gather around him. Starting at the top of the list, he calls out a name, the person approaches, and Ernesto gives him a ticket in exchange for ten pesos. After he has called out the first 100 names and distributed all of the tickets, Ernesto continues to read off the names, giving each person a share of the money collected from the others to supplement a bought ticket. For example, if there are 150 names on the list, the last fifty receive twenty pesos each to offset the cost of a forty-peso ticket.

Even though their ticket or their monetary supplement are already assured by their position on the list, most of the porra members gather in a tight circle around Ernesto, as if receiv-ing a ticket depended upon their proximity, straining to observe the proceedings in the center over their companions shoul-ders and listening carefully for their names. Again, some jok-ing mediates the seriousness of this anxiety over receiving a ticket. Some porra members shout out comic insults at the per-son being called. Others make fun of the whole situation and in particular its clientelistic overtones by making sheep sounds (*baa, baa*) or by imitating chants used in political protests, com-monly seen as shows of loyalty rather than genuine expressions of opposition by citizens.[4] Although these chants influence the porra members' attitudes in relation to the ticket distribution process, causing them to become aware of and laugh at their seriousness, the chants do not change the process itself or the facts that Ernesto maintains control and that many of the porra members could not afford to attend all of the games without the subsidized tickets. Ernesto's control of the tickets is more than a formality because he sets apart completely free tickets for his consentidos and because he alone makes the final decision as to who is or is not a member whose name can be added to the list. While such decisions rarely have to be made, when they do, involving aspiring members or members who have missed a lot of games, porra members claim that Ernesto uses the objective criteria of attendance to veil his personalized preferences (see chapter 2).

After getting their ticket, the porra members find their closest friends, with whom they will sit in the stadium, and head toward the gate. At the gate, stadium security searches knapsacks and other bags for items considered dangerous: weapons, alcohol, glass bottles, and metals cans. After a walk up a wide cement ramp, they enter the upper deck of the stadium at one end.

Once inside, a glance downward toward the field reveals a clay-red track that rings the bright green of the soccer pitch. On the field, a few players warming up share the space with a giant inflatable soccer ball with the Nike swoosh and a giant inflatable can of Mundet apple-flavored soda. The fans already in the stadium are producing a loud buzz, which will soon be accompanied by the porra's cheers. A dry moat and a set of spikes separate the track from the small lower deck, where the seats are more expensive and the experience dull, according to porra members. The large upper deck hangs over and dominates the lower one. At the ends of the stadium, the upper deck is only a few rows deep, but on both sides it gradually rises to a high peak at midfield. The stands are made of unpainted cement, but the fans' banners, flags, and clothing add plenty of color. The fans of the opposing team occupy the slightly smaller side, which is on their left as the porra members enter. The blue and gold colors of the home fans fill the other side of the stadium. After they enter, the porra members, caught up in the excitement of the quickly filling stadium, hurry toward their section near midfield at the lowest part of the upper deck.

Figure 2. The Porra Plus during a pregame warm-up in 1996, with the cheerleader supporting himself on the speaker post.

The Game

Soon after they settle into their places near their closest friends, the porra members begin interacting with the players warming up on the field and with the opposing fans in the stands on the opposite side of the stadium. Juan, an energetic and charismatic young porra member with a bellowing voice, takes his place at *el poste* (the post). He stands in front of the porra on the one-meter wall that lines the edge of the upper deck, holding onto the speaker pole beside him for support. Ernesto and his consentidos sit just in front of Juan. While Juan has some freedom to decide which cheers to initiate and when, he generally follows Ernesto's instructions. After he has taken his place, Juan makes a hand gesture for the rest of the porra members to stand. They rise from where they are sitting on the tops of the cement backrests and stand on the seat of the cement benches. Cupping one hand around his mouth to project his voice throughout the porra's section, Juan yells, ¡*Pumas, saluden a la Plus*! (Pumas, greet the Plus!). He then counts to three with his hand and the porra members repeat the phrase, shouting in unison, so that they can be heard throughout the stadium. A few of the players wave at the porra from down on the field, and the porra members clap, whistle, and shout in appreciation of the players who waved and in appreciation of their own power to create effects on the field. The players that regularly respond are those who the porra members consider *cuates* (buddies; literally fraternal twins), players they claim most fully embody and share with the fans the Pumas' ideal.

Juan then leads the porra in a similar call for a greeting from the Pumas' coach. Then, he directs the group to the opposing coach: ¡*Saluda . . . pero a tu puta madre*! (Greet . . . but to your whore mother!). This comment elicits laughter from many of the porra members, while reminding them of the real hatred and disgust they feel for the opposing team. Individual members *mientan la madre* (mention the mother; a euphemism for the insult, *chinga a tu madre*, fuck your mother) to the opposing coach, players, and fans by violently performing the obscene gesture of raising an arm, bending it almost completely at the elbow, and shaking the clenched fist back and forth. They do so in the spirit of el desmadre: angrily, yet finishing with a mocking smile on their faces. In many contexts of daily life, this insult would constitute a challenge to the male recipient's honor. To avoid losing the respect of all present, he would have to meet the challenge with an insult of his own. In this case, however, when an opposing player loses his cool and returns the obscene gesture, the porra members, rather than respecting him for taking up the challenge, deride him for taking it and himself too seriously.

After a few minutes, when everyone has settled down, Juan gets up again and shouts, ¡*Una Goya*! ¡*Una Goya*!, referring to the team cheer, as he turns his head from one side to the other to make sure that everyone gets the message.[5] Juan counts to three and then the porra members shout in unison:

Goya, Goya
Cachún, cachún, ra, ra
Cachún, cachún, ra, ra
Goya
¡Universidad!⁶

Especially if they perform La Goya loudly with the sound echoing back from the opposite side of the stadium, the porra members clap, shout, and whistle to cheer the team and their own effort.

During the half an hour or so before the game starts and then throughout the game, Juan continues to lead the porra in the shouting of insults and comments directed at opposing players and of cheers such as La Goya. Ernesto and his consentidos think up the insults and comments and pass them onto Juan. A few other porra members who sit in various sections of the stadium have the authority, developed through their relationship to Ernesto, their time as members of the porra, and their charisma, to suggest comments to Ernesto either by shouting them down to him or by passing a written note. Some porra members complain, however, that Ernesto ignores their suggestions because they are not on his list of consentidos. The wittiness of these comments is a source of pride for the porra members, who see themselves as upholders of what they consider a particularly Mexican form of expression. Thus, many express frustration regarding Ernesto's control over which comments are used, stating that the fact that his choices are based on who suggests the comment, rather than its qualities, detracts from their performance.

Generally speaking, the most frequent targets of insults are foreign players,⁷ players who have said something negative about the Pumas players or fans in the press, those most closely associated with Televisa, and former Pumas players who have turned their backs on the Pumas, at least according to the fans. The comments use word plays or *albures* (sexual double entendres) to make fun of players' nationalities, physical features, or sexual insufficiencies. For example, they tease a Colombian player on one team about being a drug dealer. They make fun of the slight stature of a Chilean player: "He takes the bus, because he does not reach *el metro*" (meaning the subway and also a meter). They symbolically cuckold an América player who had a relationship with a Televisa actress by stating that she needed a Pumas player to satisfy her sexually. They also take frequent advantage of the fact that one of the Pumas player's last name is Sancho, a name used in informal speech to refer to a man who is sleeping with a married woman: ¡*Sancho está con tu esposa!* (Sancho is with your wife). They also encourage the team or individual favorite players with statements such as, *La Plus está contigo* (the Plus is with you), occasionally eliciting a wave from the player.

Just before the beginning of the game, the players line up on the field and the porra members remove their hats and become solemn as the university's song is played over the loudspeakers.[8] Immediately after the song finishes, Juan leads them in a Goya. A few minutes later, when the ball is put into play, he leads them in another Goya. During the course of the game, there are other events on the field that require Juan to lead particular cheers. For example, after the Pumas have come close to or actually do score a goal, he calls for another Goya. When the Pumas are awarded a corner kick, a direct kick, or a penalty, he leads a long, extended cry of ¡*goooooooool!* (goal!), which is finished when the ball is kicked into play. When an opposing player leaves the game, he directs the porra in a cheer of *Te vas . . . pero a chingar a tu madre* (You're going . . . but to fuck your mother).

Besides leading the porra members in their cheers, Juan also attempts to motivate them to cheer and to cheer more passionately and loudly. When the Pumas are playing well and the game is close, there is little need for this motivation. However, when the game is near the end and the Pumas are playing badly and losing by more than one goal, porra members do not cheer with the same enthusiasm. When this occurs, Juan yells that they are there to support the team, and he insults the porra members by comparing them to old men or women. However, these efforts only slightly and temporarily increase the intensity of the cheering.

Led by Juan, and indirectly by Ernesto, porra members continue throughout the game to shout cheers such as La Goya and to yell insults at the opposing players and fans and compliments at the Pumas players. At the same time, however, another set of practices builds in intensity among the young porra members: they joke among themselves, roughhouse, and start singing and jumping up and down. These two cheering practices come into conflict. As I discuss in the next section, however, this conflict is not just a question of competing cheering styles, but rather a struggle over the group's social form and its project.

Conflicting Cheering Styles, Conflicting Modes of Sociality

When the outcome of the game is still to be determined or if the Pumas are winning, most of the porra members shout everything that Juan initiates. In addition, *apoyan al equipo* (they support the team) in a distinctive manner, including chanting, singing, and jumping up and down. For example, they break into chants of *Él que no brinque es puto* (He who doesn't jump is a fag) over and over, while putting their arms over their neighbors' shoulders and jumping up and down. To this jumping they add swaying from side to side, until members start to lose their balance and fall off of the benches, often taking those in rows below along with them. They also break into *cánticos* (songs) composed by adding lyrics about themselves and the team to the tune of popular songs and by "Puma-izing" and "Mexicanizing" songs sung by fans in Europe and South America that they hear on television. An example of a popular song with adapted lyrics goes:

¿Cómo no te voy a querer?	How could I not love you?
¿Cómo no te voy a querer?	How could I not love you?
Así mi corazón azul y	With my blue heart and my
mi piel dorada	golden skin[9]

One of the simpler adaptations of songs commonly sung by soccer fans in Europe and South America, but that I did not hear among any other fans in Mexico, goes:

> Olé,
>
> Olé olé olé,
>
> Pumas,
>
> Pumas

As they repeat the short song a few times, the porra members put their arms over each other's shoulders and sway from side to side. Usually, individual porra members invent these songs alone or with a couple of others at home between games. At other times, the invention is collective and playful as part of el cotorreo on bus trips to away games or at the occasional party where some of the porra members gather. Porra members are pleased to use fans' songs from Europe and South America (in particular Argentina, Chile, and Brazil) because they view Mexicans to be unenthusiastic soccer fans in comparison. By adopting these songs they also hope to adopt these other fans' enthusiasm and constant singing style. This adoption parallels their frequent demonstration, through hairstyles, dress, and choice of music, of a stronger connection to transnational youth cultures than to Mexicanness. The porra members insist, however, that while drawing on these fan and youth cultures from elsewhere, they always add their own creative and particularly Mexican touches.[10]

As I mentioned in the previous chapter, the young, male porra members claim that these forms of supporting the team that they initiate are truly compatible with their ideal mode of sociality. For example, in contrast to the cheers such as La Goya and the witty insults led by Juan, they claim that their songs constitute a better means of expressing their heartfelt emotion for the team. One reason they give is that it is possible to repeat the songs over and over and thus to sing throughout the game, whereas the cheers and witty insults are interspersed with breaks. They also prefer the songs because they compose them, so that the songs' content and the creative effort of the composition—not just their performance—convey their love for the team. For example, they complain that most of the insults try to get a laugh by finishing with *y chinga a tu madre* (and fuck your mother), which is only funny the first couple of times and which hardly begins to capture what they wish to express. They attribute the prevalence of this boring style to Mexico's lack of real soccer culture in contrast to Europe and South America, where fans care more about the team and the game than the wittiness of their insults. Furthermore, the porra members claim that using the same cheers or even the same songs over and over results in rote repetition without feeling, whereas the constant introduction of new compositions keeps their cheering meaningful and fresh. They also insist that their own initiation of these activities in itself is highly compatible with their ideal mode of sociality, because only in this manner, as opposed to following Juan's lead, can they sing the songs that truly reflect what they wish to express at a particular moment. They explain that they have to put up with being told what to do and being reprimanded at home, school, and work, and that this is precisely what they want to escape in the stadium. They assert that motivation for their cheering must come from the heart and cannot be commanded from above.

Before a game, a few porra members who have come up with a new song have already started to teach it to their closest friends. At some point during the game, the composers start to sing the new song. The others who already know it join in. Because the songs are short with simple lyrics and familiar tunes, other porra members learn the song quickly and can start to sing along after a couple of repetitions. This does not always occur, however. Sometimes, others do not join and those trying to initiate the song give up and stop. Whether an attempt to start a song is successful seems to depend upon a few different factors. The song's attraction for porra members at that moment is one significant factor. If the song is too new, too old, or was never very well liked, it is less likely other members will join in.

At a certain peak moment in a song's life, the porra members will always take it up right away. What is occurring during the game is also a determining factor. If porra members become distracted by a potential scoring opportunity by either team, they will less likely take up the song.

It also matters who initiates the song. If a group of porra members initiates a song together by agreeing to do so beforehand, it is more likely that other members will join in. Or, if one of the group's informal charismatic leaders does the initiating, it is also more likely to be taken up by others. By charismatic, I mean they have intangible qualities that make them leaders among their peers: when they initiate a song, they appear to be initiating it on the part of the porra as a whole. When a less charismatic member tries to initiate a song, he seems to be imposing his individual will on the porra—an act that will at best be ignored and at worst will meet with mockery and rejection. For example, if a member unsuccessfully tries to start a song, other members may surround him and force his head downward with their hands while shouting, ¡*Tri-bu-tó*! ¡*Tri-bu-tó*! (Tribute! Tribute!). The victim is physically, but playfully, forced to give a tribute of mock oral sex to pay for his foolishness. Thus, the threat of such teasing discourages most porra members from ever attempting to initiate a song. It is important to emphasize that even the most charismatic porra members can never command or force the others to sing a song. And, even if most of the members have started singing, they do not attempt to make a member who does not want to sing join in. If a porra member were to try to force others to sing or to do anything else, he would be ignored or teased by the others and might lose some of their respect upon which his informal leadership depends. I can recall one occasion when a charismatic leader started yelling angrily at porra members who were paying more attention to a nearby television camera filming them than to the game. Not only did they ignore him and continue to focus on the camera, another charismatic leader quieted him and made him look foolish by telling him not to cry over it.

The fact that porra members do not want to be commanded to sing a song does not mean that they desire some sort of a right to "individual choice" when it comes to what songs they will sing. Nor would porra members want to break up the flow and excitement of the game to vote as a group on what songs they will sing. Instead of a conscious decision or choice, the porra members want their actions to spontaneously emerge from their emotions. They want to be swept up in the excitement and emotion of the game. This particular desire seems to mediate the apparent contradiction between free individual expression and inequality implied by the existence of informal leaders. These leaders seem to be those who can best anticipate, or at least appear to anticipate, but also help to create the group's moods and desires, in such a way that the members do not have to feel commanded by them, but rather feel that they are facilitating their emotive expression. This is not to say that porra members never resent these inequalities, but because the leaders never impose their cheers and the other members can claim the right to initiate cheers themselves, there is little that can be said or done in opposition.

These contrasts between the cheering initiated by Ernesto and Juan versus the other porra members' self-initiated cheering parallel those they draw with fans of other teams. This parallel goes beyond the cheering itself to the contrast they claim exists between their ideal mode of sociality and that which Ernesto attempts to impose on them in the stadium: a hierarchical, authoritarian mode in which action is guided by others and by external objectives (the support of the team) and not by the actor's own emotions. In the stadium, this contrast takes the form of conflict when, inevitably, the two manners of supporting the team begin to interfere with each other. During a game, when the porra members first break into their chants and cheers, neither Juan nor Ernesto oppose them, and, in fact, Juan often joins in jumping up and down at his position at el poste. At some point, however, just as Juan is beginning to initiate a cheer, a group of porra members breaks into a chant or song that quickly catches on among the whole group and drowns out Juan's effort, or else a few members continue to follow his lead, inharmoniously dividing the porra's efforts. After this happens a few times, Juan grows frustrated and first pleads with and then, as his aggravation mounts, shouts at the porra members to pay attention to his lead. These shouts rarely produce the desired results. Instead, they remind them of the hierarchy that Ernesto is trying to impose. The porra members either ignore Juan, continuing to sing their songs, or they deride him for losing his temper and taking things too seriously. Eventually, Ernesto speaks up and defends Juan's position, usually at halftime when there is a break from the action. He scolds the porra members for interfering with his and Juan's attempt to organize the cheering in a coordinated and thus most effective manner. Ernesto's intervention usually quiets them for a moment—his authority, after all, is based on a real control of resources—but it does not convince them, and they recommence their own style of support. According to the porra members, Ernesto and Juan are the ones interfering, because these leaders' externally imposed cheering threatens to limit their spontaneous expression of heartfelt emotion. As I will discuss further in chapters 4 and 5, their defense against this interference is not direct, particularly with Ernesto. Rather, their main tactic is to avoid confrontation and to wear him down by continuing their style of cheering during the heat of the game when Ernesto cannot easily oppose them.

Ernesto also employs more indirect tactics in this conflict such as the incorporation of songs composed by the young porra members into the repertoire of cheers that he asks Juan to lead. This has the momentary effect of satisfying the club members' desire for a new song, partly assuaging the conflict. While these songs are still new and fresh, the porra members sing them with passion, so that their collective voice, coordinated by Juan, bellows throughout the stadium. The porra members do not mind that Juan is telling them when to sing the song, because they are still happy to sing it at any time. In fact, at these moments even the younger male porra members appreciate how Juan's direction helps to coordinate their cheering so that it is unified and louder. However, Ernesto's learning and incorporation of the songs does not keep pace with the porra members' introduction of new ones, so that, after a few games, the porra members grow tired of the song, but Juan and Ernesto have it firmly established in their repertoire. At this point, having Juan lead the song fuels rather than calms the conflict. What is at stake in this conflict for both Ernesto and the young porra members is not just a style of supporting the team, although this is undoubtedly important for all concerned, but rather whole manners of organizing social relations and action. Ernesto attempts to maintain a hierarchical arrangement culminating in his leadership, aimed at effectively supporting the team or at least appearing to do so, while the porra members struggle to create what they see as an ideal atmosphere of freedom for the expression of heartfelt emotion.

After the Game

When the game ends, regardless of its outcome, Juan calls for a Goya to celebrate the team's effort. If the team has won, a couple of the players usually acknowledge La Goya and the porra's support with a wave, eliciting cheers of appreciation from the club members. Sometimes Juan leads them in a request for a Goya directed at an individual player, usually one considered a "friend" of the porra. Juan usually does this when the player is close to the stands, either because he is being interviewed on the sidelines or he is entering the tunnel that leads to the locker room, which opens onto the field almost directly in front of the porra's section. A request for La Goya during an interview is a challenge directed at the player and a test of the porra's influence: Is the player willing to recite La Goya just after the interview while still on camera, thereby broadcasting his loyalty to the team in a context usually limited to the player's self-portrayal as a modest professional and not as a passionate Puma? If the player responds to the request, especially after the interview, he is met with enthusiastic cheers. If not, Juan continues to have them repeat the request until he obliges, acknowledges the group with a wave, or leaves the stadium. Almost half of the time, the players leave the stadium without even looking up and acknowledging the porra. Most members take this passive rejection without comment, although a few may shout out, calling the player *un mamón* (literally, a suckling), which refers to someone who appears ridiculous because he thinks and acts as if he were superior to others and thus has no need for them.

After the players have left the field, Ernesto gathers the members to fix a meeting time for the next home game and the next away game if they are planning to attend as a group. He may also use the gathering to scold the porra members for their disorderly behavior and for disrupting the group's coordinated cheering. On occasions when there is a need for a longer and more involved meeting, such as when an election for an official position in the porra is required or when a conflict has arisen between Ernesto and some of the young members (see chapter 5), Ernesto calls for the members to gather in the area of the parking lot where they meet before games.

By the time the porra members leave the stadium, usually about twenty or thirty minutes after the game has ended, it is empty except for the soda and beer salesmen putting away their wares. As they head back to the same area of the parking lot, the mood is partially determined by the results of the game, but even after a loss they continue to cotorrear and enjoy each other's company. Back in the parking lot, someone takes up a collection to buy a soccer ball from one of the remaining paraphernalia vendors. The almost disposable balls are cheap, costing only thirty pesos. Two small goals are set up in the nearly empty parking lot about thirty meters apart. The cement playing area is almost without boundaries and a chase for the ball may lead players to the edges of the parking lot and around parked cars and other obstacles. Two porra members begin to alternate making selections for their team. There is little worry, however, over the evenness of the teams in terms of either numbers or ability, although a tally of goals scored is kept. Players constantly leave

Figure 3. A pickup soccer game in the stadium parking lot.

the game, which lasts about an hour, sometimes to chat with the porra members who are not playing and sometimes to head home. If they re-enter the game, it may even be with the other team if that side is losing players more quickly.

By the time the game ends, just five or six players are left of the thirty or so who originally crowded the makeshift pitch. They then join the few remaining porra members not in the game who are standing nearby joking around and chatting. At this point, there is little need to create the porra members' ideal mode of sociality. Rather, the remaining porra members' efforts are aimed at doing what they can to extend it into the late hours of the Sunday afternoon, putting off going home to their families and to work or school the next day. There are few options open, however, in terms of available and affordable spaces and activities for the porra members to continue.

No one bothers them in the empty parking lot, however, even when they take up a collection to buy a bottle of brandy, some sodas for mixing, and some plastic cups in the nearby

UNAM employees' union grocery store. The remaining ten or so members find a shaded corner of the parking lot to sit in, sip their *cubas* (the term for a rum and coke, extended to all drinks mixed with soda), and reflect upon the day's game. They also recall exaggerated tales of shared past adventures on trips to away games, interspersed with the usual cotorreo of teasing and insults. As they get drunker, conversations turn into debate over a variety of issues from soccer to politics. The effects of the alcohol mediate the seriousness of these debates, framing them as a sort of serious play, like a debating competition or chess match. Three or four hours after the game, perhaps as the sun starts to set, the hungry and tired hangers-on reluctantly board a bus to head home. In the bus and then on the subway, they continue to chat, sometimes now about upcoming games, but the group rapidly diminishes as the porra members split off at subway stops to head to different parts of the city.

Female Porra Members and Gendered Tensions

During the game, the five or six women who go to the stadium unaccompanied by a brother, husband, or boyfriend sit together near the front of the porra's section, with Ernesto and his followers in front of them and the rowdier young male fans behind. They participate in most of the group's cheers and songs. However, they occasionally remain seated instead of standing and jumping up and down like their male counterparts, and they sometimes abstain from the witty insults with sexual innuendos. While many of the men make comments to those around them regarding exceptional plays by the Pumas players, a lack of effort on the part of Pumas players, and bad calls by the umpires against the Pumas, the women tend to comment on the relationship between how a player has been feeling mentally and physically and his performance. When one of their favorite players comes out onto the field from the locker room, enters the game, or makes a good play, the young women express excitement, sometimes joking that he is her *novio* (boyfriend).

After the game and the group's brief meeting, with the help of Ernesto's influence, they go into the locker rooms to greet (*saludar*) the players and to congratulate or console them. For the female porra members being a fan involves discussing their likes and dislikes of the players as soccer players and as people as well as talking to them after games or practices to get to know them personally. As one female fan explained, "It's great to come to the stadium and even better when you get to know the players. Then, you come for what each of the players means to you, and your emotions for the team increase a lot." The women claim that through their personal contact with the players they are able to encourage them and thereby support the team. Beyond the post-game locker-room visits, they also attend the team's practices whenever they are able to during the week, which for some of them means almost every day. They go to watch the training and to talk to the players at the end of the practice, as the players walk to their cars while signing autographs. Because these porra members consider themselves the players' friends, however, they do not ask for autographs. From these interactions, which differ in length and quality from player to player, the female porra members claim that they are able to ascertain the different personalities of the players, how the players are feeling on a particular day or week, and how well they get along personally with each player. For example, a female fan explained to me during an interview that certain players were her favorites (*consentillidos*)[11] "because they are very straightforward. They are guys who truly fight for what they want. They have a lot of character, and they know how to respect someone who respects them." The female porra members' overall opinions of players consist of a combination of their evaluation of personal interactions and evaluations of a player's playing ability and his physical attractiveness.

The Men's Views of the Women

Most of the male porra members shun the idea of entering the locker room or talking at any length with the players after their practices. They criticize this as a form of worship, an act of going to give tribute to the players that parallels a clientelistic relationship. They claim to be the players' equals, perhaps not on the field, but as youths and people. Furthermore, they state that as equals they wish to respect the players' privacy and thus do not want to bother them after a game or practice. Sometimes, the male porra members do head over to the side of the stadium where the players come out from the locker room after games and walk toward their cars. When the players they consider *cuates* emerge, an individual member may greet them with a brief wave, a thumbs-up if the team won, or a handshake if the player passes close enough and is not mobbed by other fans looking for autographs. The male porra members are careful to show little emotion: their movements are understated and their voices calm. Too much excitement leads to teasing that they like the player in a romantic sense.

The choice of the term "cuate" instead of "amigo," which the women use to describe their relationships to the players, is significant. Anthropologist Larissa Lomnitz (1977) noted that among men in a marginal neighborhood in Mexico City cuate refers to a particularly close friendship compared to the term amigo. My research, however, conducted nearly thirty years later among these soccer fans as well as gangs of street youth, suggests a shift in meaning among male porra members as well as other men in the city, who avoid the term amigo because of its connotations of a romantic relationship, originating in the use of *amiga* (female friend) to refer to a lover (as opposed to a girlfriend, *una novia*, or a wife, *esposa/mujer*). They use *cuate*, in contrast, to signal an emotional distance even to the friends with whom they spend the most time. Thus, the use of cuate to refer to players with whom they get along well derives from and contributes to an overall situation in which the expression of strong feelings for the team, the game, and their ideal vision is positively evaluated among their male peers. In contrast, any expression of feelings regarding individual players is looked down upon and mocked.

The male porra members do not tease the women in their

presence. However, when talking among themselves about the women's practices, they mock them and even express anger. They joke that the women are so ugly that they probably scare the players when trying to talk to them, and they speculate that the players must feel annoyed at having to talk to the female porra members so often. Only half-joking, they suggest that the players' experience of being frightened or annoyed by the female porra members causes them physical or psychological trauma that then worsens their performance on the field. The male porra members complain that besides asking for the occasional auto-graph, their female counterparts should not bother the players, because the players are not interested in them romantically or sexually. One porra member justified this reasoning by explain-ing to me, "I don't try to ask out models and actresses because I know that they aren't interested in me, and I would just be bothering them and wasting their time. For the same reason, they shouldn't bother the players." Thus, overall, the male porra members portray their female counterparts' actions as attempts to initiate romantic relationships with the players and represent the women themselves as too unattractive for the players to even consider responding.

The male porra members extend these portrayals to the female porra members' interactions with them as well. Upon observing one of the female porra members initiating an inter-action with one of the men, they might make a joke, with other male porra members as their audience, referring to the woman's unattractiveness and her attempts to *atrapar* (capture) the male porra member in a romantic sense. For example, they some-times jokingly refer to these women as *arañas* (spiders), imply-ing their ability to capture unsuspecting victims. On occasions, in a more serious tone, one of them would warn me to beware of the female members, although I was not able to get them to specify why. Whenever a male porra member shows or admits romantic interest in one of the female members, the others tease him, usually until he withdraws his earlier admission and stops demonstrating any feelings to the contrary.

A similar vigilance extends to dyadic relationships between

male friends. Almost all of the porra members consider some or many of their fellow porra members to be cuates, but if two of the male porra members are seen to always do everything together, such as sit together in the stadium and talk together in the parking lot, other porra members begin to tease them by framing their relationship as a romantic one. For example, if one of them were to appear without the other at any moment, they might ask him where his *amante* (lover) was. During the first half of my fieldwork, José Luis and César appeared to be very close friends and could always be found together during the porra's activities. However, after withstanding a couple of months of teasing from other porra members about their close friendship, I noticed that the two of them started spending less time together, at which point the teasing stopped.

While the stigma of homosexuality is used to break apart close dyadic relationships, I do not believe that homosexuality is the porra members' real preoccupation, considering that heterosexual relationships are attacked in a similar manner. In fact, I was never able to get them to voice their "real preoccupation" over these two types of relationship, so I must admit some uncertainty about the explanation I am about to suggest. These misogynistic and homophobic tendencies seem to be products of the male porra members seeing these dyadic relationships as a threat to their ideal mode of sociality, in a manner parallel to their preoccupation with clientelistic relationships. They view these dyadic relationships, but particularly the heterosexual ones, not only as incompatible with the freedom necessary for individual expression, but as sufficiently comprehensive and binding to draw them away from the porra and its sociality. There is some evidence that the threat represented by these relationships is real. On a couple of occasions, I observed that porra members' attendance diminished soon after getting married, although this is by no means a general pattern. Furthermore, porra members only rarely bring their girlfriends or wives to the games and when they do there is a noticeable social distance between the couple and the male porra members around them.

Although the male porra member continues to cheer and sing with the group, he does not participate in the roughhousing and casual joking going on around him. This is not a distance based on antagonism but more likely on a shared recognition that the porra member is not fully participating in the group's activities because his attention is partly directed toward his partner and hers is on him and his behavior.

I should state that porra members themselves do not admit to any such general preoccupation over "women," "marriage," or "friendship" in general. Thus, I may simply be wrong, and their denigration of the female porra members may have a cause other than the threat of close dyadic relationships that I think these women represent for them. Perhaps, for example, they are jealous over the fact that the women direct their attention to the players and not to them. However, I think that there's a reason why they would not want to admit such a general preoccupation even if it did exist. As men, it is in their interest to portray themselves as unthreatened by women, marriage, or friendships because representing these as threats would imply that women or their own feelings for another could dominate them. Male porra members can admit to clientelism as a threat without implying their own individual weakness because it is viewed as a general social problem with the power to dominate nearly a whole nation (of men). Obedience to or dominance by emotions such as love or women, however, are attributed to the individual characters, or more specifically weaknesses, of particular men. The connection the male porra members draw between commitment to dyadic relationships and weakness is revealed in the content of their teasing when they chide other men for showing romantic interest in one of the women or for forming a close friendship with another man. Simple statements such as ¿Dónde está tu novia/novio? (Where's your girlfriend/boyfriend?) are meant to suggest a done deed—something the victim of the teasing can do nothing about because he is the passive object of his emotional needs.

Other students of urban Mexican men's portrayals of their

relationships to women have noted a similar avoidance of admitting emotion needs. For example, Stanley Brandes (2002:124–25) in his ethnographic study of an Alcoholics Anonymous group in Mexico City noted that the men tend to end their stories of interactions with women on a note of sexual conquest, attempting to signal their masculine prowess. In the case of the male porra members, their displacement of the "threat" onto individual women's supposed unattractiveness shields them from appearing weak, susceptible, and less manly. I believe that the real threat, however, is the relationships and social contexts that men and not just women are interested in: romantic relationships and domesticity.

My research on gangs of street youths in Mexico City revealed how men confront a similar tension between an all-male social context (the gang) and the romantic/domestic sphere (Magazine 2004a). Both the gang and their romantic/domestic relationships with women make demands on the young men's limited resources. Consequently, they feel pulled in opposite directions and know that they cannot fulfill obligations in both sets of relationships. Individual men deal with the problem in different ways, but one common reaction is to blame their wives and girlfriends for trying to control them, which in turn may be used to justify physical and verbal abuse. As among the porra members, however, the romantic/domestic leanings are their own, and placing blame on women may be a way to externalize an internal conflict.

There is also evidence of similar tensions between all-male social contexts and romantic/domestic relations in the historical record. Ilene O'Malley (1986:134), for example, in her history of hero cults in postrevolutionary Mexico, reported such a notion in a literary portrayal of Pancho Villa: "One of the most startling examples of the primacy of male relationships occurred in the novel *Vámonos con Pancho Villa*. Tiburcio's profoundest attachment was to Villa; his wife and children were only impediments. Villa also saw them as impediments, and so he killed them. But he killed only Tiburcio's girl child; he spared the boy because he too could become a villista."[12] While in this case there is little effort to hide the source of the threat, more commonly, portrayals of women are similar to the porra members' in that they divert attention from women's power as romantic or domestic partners and from men's own emotions, excluding them without explicitly admitting to their status as "impediments" or threats. Elena Poniatowska interviewed participants in the 1968 student movement in Mexico aimed against the government's authoritarian practices. She quoted at least two men, a writer and a sociologist, who question women's participation in the movement because they had not even challenged their own submission to authority in the home (1971:95–96). Such statements could be read as a general preoccupation over the infiltration of the domestic sphere into the movement, while singling out women as the culprits diverts attention from men's own domestic influences and leanings.

This diversion has usually taken the form of portraying women as either whores or as sexually chaste mothers, thereby denying them agency of any other type, including their agency as lovers and wives. In reference to the romantic period in Mexican literature, Margarita Vargas (1994:93–94) noted:

> Thus, in romanticism, the bipolar myth, Virgin/Eve, works to emphasize the virtues to which all women should aspire and to denigrate those women who fail to conform. In either case, the mutual exclusivity of the two options, the lack of any medial ground, restricts the possible lives of women: on the one hand, although to live as a Virgin integrates a woman into society, it denies a large part of her being; on the other hand, to lead a free life of the Malinche automatically ostracizes her from society.[13]

As suggested by Vargas, this bipolar myth, frequently represented by the figures of the Malinche (an indigenous woman portrayed in national mythology as having prostituted herself and her people to the Spanish conqueror Cortés) and the Virgin of Guadalupe, aims to exclude women's full participation and, I would add, domesticity in general from Mexican public life, imagined as a collectivity of Mexican *men*. Jean Franco (1989:146) reached a similar conclusion through her own study of Mexican literature: "Women's attempts to plot themselves as protagonists in the national novel become a recognition of the fact that they are not in the plot at all but definitely somewhere else."

Women who challenge this exclusion are portrayed as promiscuous and thus as a moral threat. For example, Elaine Carey, in her book on the 1968 student movement in Mexico, found that women who took on public roles in the movement, roles generally reserved for men, were automatically assumed to be sexually active and under insidious foreign influence (Carey 2005). The male porra members do not go so far as to portray their female counterparts as whores, although their idea that the women are only interested in the players as potential boyfriends does serve to reduce their agency and fandom to a single, exaggerated dimension. As I will show in the next chapter, the male members do employ the elements of this bipolar myth, in particular the Eve pole, in relation to women they confront as strangers, suggesting, as others already have (e.g., Melhuus 1998), that the bipolar myth is still significant, although not uncontested, today.

Street youths and Pancho Villa's army hardly share the porra members' Romantic ideal vision for Mexican society. The participants in the 1968 student movement have more in common with the porra members, although there are significant differences between the two groups and their outlooks on life. The street youths and the participants in the student movement are similar in terms of age to the porra members, while the members of Villa's army were not necessarily youths. Therefore, it seems likely that the tension experienced by male porra members between all-male relations versus romantic/domestic relations is a product not of their Romantic ideal vision or of their youthfulness but rather of something common to all of these social contexts. Although I will not try to define that something, I will point out that this tension parallels a broader ideology, with its origins in the modern West (Strathern 1988), that values the public sphere over the private and emphasizes men's participation in the former while downplaying their role in the latter.[14] I posit that the emergence in a given social context of all-male or male-dominated social groupings such as armies, youth gangs, or the porra that are perceived as distinct and separate from— as opposed to being complementary to—the domestic sphere is somehow tied to the prevalence of this broader ideology. If this is the case, then such attempts to exclude romantic desires and domesticity from all-male social contexts and achieving this exclusion by scapegoating women are by no means unique to Mexico. It is also important to add that this broader ideology and the existence of such all-male groups do not always produce tensions with the domestic sphere. I would venture to say that such tensions arise under conditions of duress, such as when a lack of resources makes it difficult for men to fulfill both sets of obligations, as in the case of the street youths or Villa's army, or when a specific all-male group is in a precarious state and thus requires the undivided loyalty of its members to survive, such as in the cases of Villa's army, the 1968 student movement, and the porra. It would be interesting to test this explanation by investigating whether the eighteenth- and nineteenth-century European Romantic movement, which suffered from the precariousness that comes with challenging dominant forces, involved such tensions.

Whatever the reason for this criticism and mocking of the female porra members, the women's own explanations reveal that, while the male porra members correctly sense that the women do not share their interests, they lack a clear understanding of what the female porra members are actually doing. During interviews, female porra members explained that their primary reasons for coming to the stadium are that they like soccer and they truly feel something for the team. They state that coming to see the players as imaginary *novios* (boyfriends) is just something extra. Furthermore, they claim that what was most important to them in their relations to porra members and to the players is friendship. One of them specifically pointed out that she did not want to have a boyfriend in the porra because she considered the porra members to be her friends. They specifically distinguish themselves from the young women who are not interested in soccer at all and who come to the practices or games just to throw themselves, in a sexual sense, at the players.

José Limón (1994:185) posited that when working-class Mexican-American women in South Texas say that they would like to dance with the handsome, well-dressed, blond, fantastic dancer who appears at bars, and who turns out to be the devil, they are creating "their version of a Bakhtinian universe of the carnivalesque, excluded as they are from other universes." They are figuratively and almost literally "dancing with the devil" as they dangerously transgress the norms of female propriety that constitute gender hierarchy. Similarly, when the female porra members talk openly about their crushes, they are playfully transgressing the boundaries of what their parents consider appropriate and safe behavior for young single women. This is their version of el desmadre (see chapter 4). A slight contrast to what Limón finds is that these women choose not to participate in the "other universes" of the porra even before the male porra members exclude them. It is interesting to note that Limón proposed that his male informants interpret the women's stories about dancing with the devil as an expression of their desire to marry wealthy Anglos (1994:175–76, 183). These men, like the male porra members, take the women's play too seriously at the same time that they misunderstand the seriousness of their play. That is, in the case under study here, the women are not serious about forming romantic relationships with the porra members or even with the players, but through their playfulness they are seriously critiquing more general social expectations that restrict their behavior to that of virgin mothers or whores, barring the possibility of expressing romantic or sexual desires in a respectable manner.

The female porra members also have different preoccupations regarding the future of the group than their male counterparts. While the men criticize clientelism in the porra and appear to worry about the infiltration of dyadic relationships, the women focus their critiques on the divisions created by the conflicts between Ernesto and the young, male porra members.

In general, the female porra members seem to share with the men the idea that the porra and Pumas fandom offer an alternative to dominant forms of sociality outside the stadium. However, whereas the men are looking for an alternative to clientelism and democratic rationality, the women are in search of an alternative to family members' expectations that they behave as virgin mothers. In this sense, the Pumas' philosophy of puros jóvenes appeals to the women because it promises, at least in theory, a lack of vigilance and control by family members and, in particular, by parents. The women's search for freedom from parental control is meaningless to the male porra members, whose parents expect them to spend time outside the house making a place for themselves in the worlds of work and politics and even *echando desmadre* (having fun, creating disorder). Meanwhile, the women do not seem particularly interested in the men's alternative social project or with their struggles against Ernesto within the group.

Another difference between the women's and the men's relationship to the Pumas and the porra stems from the fact that, whereas the women attribute their fandom and their search for an alternative to traditional gender roles to a freely made choice, the men see their fandom as beginning with imposed exclusion from the world of work and politics and culminating in a struggle to practice their ideal. Thus, for the men being a porra members means facing frustration, disappointment, and constant conflict and opposition, but the women criticize these same conflicts for their detrimental effects on the kinds of egalitarian friendships they join the porra to seek. As one female porra member lamented, "We're very divided. There are the young men, the old men, and the women all in separate groups. I would like us to be more together. You have to accept people as they are with their errors."[15]

While I do not have a definitive answer as to why the women

and men differ in their interest in and relationship to the porra and the Pumas, I do have some thoughts that might serve, at least, to initiate a discussion of this topic. I imagine that this difference in interests has something to do with the ideology concerning public and private spheres mentioned above, which encourages men to interest themselves in broad social issues related to work and politics and directs women toward concerns with concrete face-to-face relationships. More specifically, this difference in interests suggests that these young women, in comparison with the young men, may be less concerned with and involved in the crumbling of the pyramid and the emergence of alternatives forms of public sociality. I think this is due at least partially to the fact that the recent shift may have been less detrimental to women's opportunities in employment and politics, or may even have improved such opportunities in some contexts. Although the female porra members do not seem to share the men's frustration and disappointment over exclusion from work, school, and politics, I lack the necessary data to compare trends in the women's versus the men's actual employment opportunities. Other research suggests that women's employment opportunities have increased as men's have declined in neoliberal Mexico City among the working class (Benería and Roldán 1992; Gutmann 1996), but I know of no such gender-sensitive studies regarding the upwardly mobile working-class and middle-class sectors that the majority of porra members represent. In any case, I believe that independent of real opportunities for women versus men, these young women's relative lack of interest in contemporary changes in public sociality has to do with the fact that their self understandings and evaluations have less to do with positioning themselves in public socialities and more to do with specific, personal relationships such as with the players.

Obviously, the women's ideals and projects within the group and beyond deserve the same analytical attention as that of the men. Unfortunately, because of time limitations in the field as well as my efforts to maintain good relations with my male informants, my data on the female porra members are limited. Here I hoped to show that, although there is a significant gap between the men's and the women's interests, the men's perception of the women as a problem says more about them than about the women themselves. More specifically, it shows that the men frequently reproduce patterns of behavior associated with the typical Mexican man, not because of some sort of inherent masculinity but rather as a defense against tensions between their own interests in all-male and public versus domestic modes of sociality. Meanwhile, more research is needed on Mexican women's ideas and practices in nondomestic, nonwork contexts such as soccer stadiums, streets, and nightclubs.

In this chapter, I have described how the porra members attempt to put their ideal vision for society into practice in and around the stadium, before, during, and after games. This effort involves struggle and confrontation that consist of defending their ideal vision from other modes of sociality. The domesticity supposedly represented by the female porra members constitutes one threat, although the main impediments parallel the dominant forces at the national level: neoliberal democracy and clientelism. My objective in this chapter has been to move beyond the porra members' ideal vision to its practice and implementation, and in a somewhat parallel sense, to look beyond celebrations of an emerging democracy to the continuing presence of clientelism and coercive practices at various levels of urban Mexican society.

In the next chapter, I describe in much greater detail the practices of el desmadre, showing how they affect relationships among different categories of actors in the porra and trying to make sense of them within the wider context of the invention of tradition in twentieth-century Mexico.

4

Performing Motherlessness

Violence, Masculinity, and the Subversive Use of an Invented Tradition

My portrayal of the porra member's practices up to this point has been incomplete. I have described their practices as if they consisted exclusively of creating and living their ideal mode of sociality, a mode that permits the free expression of heartfelt emotion for the team, the game of soccer, and life in general. However, an observer of their practices before, during, or after a game would inevitably wonder what the insults directed at innocent bystanders and passersby or the burning of all flammable objects within reach have to do with this ideal mode. Precisely because these practices of apparently meaningless violence and unbridled anger seem incompatible with the porra members' well-thought-out social project, I have decided to treat them separately. In addition to filling in this ethnographic gap, my objective in this chapter is to make sense of such practices and to show how they do in fact fit into the porra members' social project, by placing them in the context of conflicts within the group and in the wider context of meanings of violence, disorder, and masculinity in twentieth-century Mexico.

The following excerpt from my field notes gives an idea of the type of practices the porra members categorize as el desmadre:

> Outside of the stadium before the game there were the usual cries of ¡Pinche ridículo! [Goddamn fool!] when América fans walked by the spot where the porra meets outside of the stadium. Inside the stadium, porra members grabbed all

América flags that came anywhere near our section. Then they ripped up or burned the flags and tied them into longer pieces that they swung around above their heads and later took home as souvenirs.

Someone noted that there was going to be more security today than usual. On the way in to the stadium, Jorge had picked up a flyer that said something like "Please maintain calm and order for the safety of yourself and your family" and at the bottom it had the Pumas and the América logos side by side. When Jorge showed it to the other guys, someone grabbed it from him and crumpled it up, while others started to chant ¡*Vio-len-cia*! ¡*Vio-len-cia*!

Someone had brought two real chicken's feet (perhaps a reference to the América mascot, an eagle), which were tossed around the section and then tied onto the ends of the América flags. Jorge, not unhappily, ended up with the blood all over his hands. Later when a few models with skimpy outfits advertising a soft drink appeared on the field, they burst out into a chant of ¡*Se-xo*! ¡*Se-xo*!, and a few individuals shouted lewd comments to the amusement of the others.

As usual in an important game, after the Pumas scored a goal, everyone jumped on top of everyone else and miraculously no one got crushed between the pile of bodies and the cement benches.

What I failed to fully capture in this field note, perhaps because it seemed unexceptional to me at the time, is the tone of these practices. While one might expect they are being performed by an angry mob—and it might even look that way from a distance—as an observer in their midst I could not miss their smiles, laughter, and mockery. In this sense, desmadre refers to "fun," but to a particular sort of fun that involves purposefully and irreverently breaking the rules. The young men in the porra are undoubtedly angry over their lack of opportunities and the modes of sociality they are often forced to live, but the vast majority of the time this is not the undisciplined anger of the mob. Rather, the members have channeled their anger into the formulation and implementation of their ideal vision and into the rule-breaking derision that I describe in this chapter. In an effort to make sense of the porra members' practices and to show how these practices fit into their social project, I explore el desmadre's standard contemporary meaning, its role in twentieth-century Mexican history, and its appropriation and inversion by young people.

The word "desmadre" literally translates as "motherlessness," but it is most commonly used to refer to a disorderly state or a mess. For example, one might say that *la casa es un desmadre* (the house is a mess) or *mi vida es un desmadre* (my life is a mess). What the English word "mess" does not fully capture, however, is the moral implication of el desmadre, which implies the lack of a mother's influence and the moral order that only that influence can bring. Therefore, to say that la casa es un desmadre conveys the idea that the state of the house offends the basic morality that only mothers can instill in their children. The meaning of another colloquial expression, *no tener madre* (to not have a mother) sheds some light on this moral state of motherlessness. To say that someone *no tiene madre* is perhaps the harshest way of saying that someone is a terrible person without morals or manners because someone who does not have a mother has not only acted immorally or rudely, they also do not feel any remorse or guilt about what they have done. For example, residents of Mexico City often find this expression useful for describing the arbitrarily abusive practices of the police. Whenever police appeared on the playing field of the stadium, porra members were likely to break into a chant of:

Chinga de noche	Fucking us by night
Chinga de día	Fucking us by day
No tiene madre la policía	The police have no mother

This chant refers to the manner in which the police abuse citizens without remorse, compassion, or consideration for the feelings of their victims because they have no moral conscience, no mother.

Figure 4. Desmadre inspired by the
camera before a game in 1997.

A Small Private Revolution:
The Invention of a National Tradition

In Argentina and Great Britain, violence (usually playful violence) among soccer fans has frequently provoked serious preoccupation among state actors and violent reprisals by police. Eduardo Archetti and Amílcar Romero (1994:38), writing about Argentina, stated that organized collective violence among fans "comes to be defined as a threat not only to the social order but also the legitimacy of the State and its legal institutions." Gary Armstrong (1998) noted that in the Great Britain of the 1980s, the media, sociologists, and the government successfully portrayed soccer fans as the cause of rising feelings of insecurity, which were in reality created by rises in unemployment and the dismantling of the welfare state. These portrayals were used to justify sophisticated surveillance systems in stadiums, police violence, and imprisonment of minor offenders.

In contrast, I observed how similar forms of playful violence among the porra members provoked a different reaction in authorities. Ernesto, for example, would admonish them for inappropriate behavior and would attempt to explain to them how they should be protecting the women and children in the stadium. To him, their actions were less a threat to the porra and its social order than a reason to take on a paternal role and finish the state's project of producing a modern citizenry capable of constituting an orderly society. To fully understand the porra members' practices as well as the specifically Mexican reaction to them, it is necessary to go beyond the meaning of the term "desmadre" to the place it occupies within the broader symbolic order through which urban Mexicans understand their own social world.[1] To do so requires a return to a process of tradition invention (Hobsbawm and Ranger, eds. 1983) begun in the years following the Mexican Revolution, through which violence, disorder, and masculinity were characterized in a particular manner.[2] In his book *La jaula de la melancholia* (*The Cage of Melancholy*), Roger Bartra (1987:33) traced this process, describing how Mexico City intellectuals invented a new version of *lo mexicano* to explain what they perceived as a continuing situation of underdevelopment in contrast to the government's claims of progress and national well-being. They explained this underdevelopment through the invention of the typical postrevolutionary Mexican, *el pelado*, and his actions, described as *el relajo*.

El pelado is the poor male migrant in the city trapped between two worlds: the primitive and the modern. Although he carries with him the primitivism of his indigenous/peasant past, he has lost touch with his traditions. The transition has been too rapid, however, and el pelado has not yet completed his conversion to proletariat in the strange new world of the industrial city. His intermediate state explains the failure of modernization efforts. Because el pelado is trapped between two worlds, he is potentially violent, dangerous, and rebellious (Bartra 1987:109).

Yet, the elite, who can avoid direct contact with el pelado, have little to fear from this violent rebelliousness—as long as it is not harnessed by a great leader—because it expresses itself not in true revolutionary action but through el relajo. El relajo is a form of action and, in particular, speech that inverts or muddles everything it comes into contact with, turning order into chaos. Thus, el relajo produces el desmadre (although in contemporary usage, "el desmadre" is often used alone to designate both the cause and the effect). Originally the term "el relajo" described an action used by the popular classes to entangle and neutralize mechanisms of domination and exploitation (Bartra 1987:163). Portrayed in the nationalist myth, however, it also entangles revolutionary channels of action. Intellectuals portrayed el relajo as the domesticated and docile version of el pelado's rebelliousness, diverting revolutionary potential into the small private revolution of humor, irony, and vulgarity (Bartra 1987:162).

For these notions to be recognizable to the majority of Mexicans, they had to be derived from or at least related to aspects of popular culture (O'Malley 1986:140; Bartra 1987:163, 195). Yet, the final version was undoubtedly a product of Mexico City intellectuals, reflecting their values and interests (Bartra 1987:190).

When this final version was returned to the general population through media, such as the movies of the comedian Cantinflas (Bartra 1987:150), the invention of a national tradition was complete. By the 1940s, el pelado and el relajo had become an idiom of Mexicanness. Yet, while critical of the government's claims of success, these portrayals served the interests of the government in at least two ways. First, these representations of a homogeneous Mexicanness, despite their critical bent, silenced the divisions in a war-torn country and obscured regional and class differences, confirming the existence of a Mexican nation, however unhealthy, which in turn served to legitimate the Mexican national government and its claims to sovereignty. Second, the primitive character of el pelado, his lack of discipline, and his childish rebelliousness called for strong, paternalistic leadership to complete his modernization. The government was the obvious candidate to take on this leadership, a position it consolidated through the creation and appropriation of revolutionary heroes such as Emiliano Zapata (O'Malley 1986).

Subsequently, this successful consolidation of a strong, paternalistic government embodied in a one-party political system with control over the institutions of civil society, such as labor unions and even private industry, led to a different preoccupation among critical intellectuals during the 1950s and 1960s. The Mexican intellectual and poet Octavio Paz (1961), for example, conceptualized the problem of Mexico's continuing failure to measure up to European and North American nations not in terms of the disorderliness and lack of discipline of its citizens but rather in terms of a national penchant for authority. According to Paz, authoritarian images of the father as both benevolent patriarch and terrible macho led Mexicans to seek these types of relationships outside the home as well. During this period of political stability, Paz voiced his belief that the psychological needs to dominate and be dominated made it impossible for Mexicans to break away from the pyramid of hierarchical relations and achieve the modern ideal of liberal democracy.

The publication of *The Cage of Melancholy* coincided with another shift in state form (Bartra 1987:17). Paz and other intellectuals had welcomed this shift as the birth of an independent civil society and a true turn to democracy. For example, the Mexican intellectual Carlos Monsiváis (1987) declared Mexico to be the "society that organizes," no longer permitting the state to escape its demands. He even painted a positive picture of the chaos that seems to permeate contemporary Mexican society, suggesting that through rituals of chaos citizens have created a space for true enjoyment (Monsiváis 1995).

As usual, other intellectuals reacted more critically to the shift, or at least with apprehension. For example, while Bartra seemed hopeful that this time around Mexicans could prevent a small group of intellectuals from inventing their traditions for them, he was concerned. According to Bartra, with the fall of these myths, the Mexican has been stripped of his past and present and lives in a world of discordances and contradictions (Bartra 1987:199). In a later article he linked this liminal state with an identity crisis (Bartra 1998:17). Expressing a similar preoccupation, historian and anthropologist Claudio Lomnitz (1996) wrote about the "fissions" in contemporary Mexican nationalism, wondering if there exists a vision for the future that can bridge the gap between the new globalized Mexico and the old closed, nationalist one.

This critical view reached its pinnacle in the writings of Mexican sociologist Sergio Zermeño. In his 1996 book, *La sociedad derrotada* (the defeated society), Zermeño argued that policy shifts since the 1980s have stripped Mexicans of their modernity, constituted by the collective identities of a strong civil society, organized through national and local business associations, proletariat unions, and peasant organizations, and have replaced it with a process of savage modernization, meant to create a new neoliberal modernity based on transnational competitiveness. According to Zermeño, while these new policies have brought about democratization at the political level, they ignore the societal level, leaving Mexicans stripped of an old civil society and without yet possessing a new one, producing pauperization, anomie, what he calls "disidentity," and, most of all, social disorder.

These recent critical visions reproduce many aspects of the earlier intellectual productions discussed by Bartra. According to these authors, the urban Mexican man is once again experiencing a crisis because he has been violently removed from an old social order, but has not yet found or adapted to a new one. This time he is not stuck between rural primitivism and urban modernity, but rather between an old nationalist modernity and a new liberal global one. My interest in these portrayals is not their accuracy, but rather their effects. Like earlier preoccupations about the nation, they invent the notion of a lost citizenry in need of guidance. Once again, these intellectual representations about the Mexican citizenry return to that citizenry and become a discourse for talking about and practicing Mexicanness and being a man in a particularly Mexican manner.

These negative representations, rather than the positive ones of authors such as Monsiváis, seem to catch on more readily as representations of national tradition, especially in Mexico City, where residents are constantly on the lookout for examples of the nation's failures. For example, people assume that apparently spontaneous popular political organization is really controlled by the government or other forces. In many social contexts within the capital, the prevalent contemporary image of Mexicanness is one of dismodernity, disorder (or in local terms, desmadre), and identity crisis.

I contend that these intellectuals, through two periods of imagining the typical Mexican during periods of political instability, one during the first half of the twentieth century and another near its end, have invented el desmadre as a national "tradition" (Hobsbawm and Ranger 1983), making it available, at least in Mexico City, as an idiom for talking about the actions of "typical" Mexican men. In the middle of these two periods was a time of relative political stability during which the idiom of "machismo" served as the invented national tradition regarding "typical" Mexican men. Along with other young men, porra members have appropriated the idiom of el desmadre in their own particular manner, inverting it and using it to describe activities that are fun, but also exciting, precisely because they break the rules, albeit in a manner that is expected and even tolerated. The appropriation of the term itself, celebrating something that is supposed to be negative, is an example of this rule-breaking fun. For porra members, watching the Pumas win or playing soccer in the parking lot after the game may be fun, but these acts are not in themselves desmadre. If we add insults shouted at the opposing team, a pile-on in the stands to celebrate a win, or some alcohol to the pick-up game, then it is desmadre.

The existence of this widely recognized tradition allows the porra members to put an additional twist on el desmadre at times, doing things or pretending to do things solely because they are what people expect of young men in crisis. I would say that porra members *perform* these things in a playful or mocking manner and require an audience to shock. Shocking onlookers adds to the fun of these activities, and sometimes the performance is a bonus added to an activity that would be fun even without an audience. For example, when the porra members jump up and down and sing during the game the fun derives directly from the defiance of the norms of bodily comportment within the stands (see below) without the need of an audience. However, they also know and enjoy the fact that they may shock and frighten onlookers. In contrast, when they shout ¡Violencia, violencia! their sole intention is to perform the role of the angry, rebellious mob and to shock an audience of onlookers. The fun comes not only from shocking the audience, which usually consists of opposing fans or bystanders in public spaces, but from mocking them as well, revealing the audience's unquestioned acceptance of national myths and their inability to distinguish between performance and reality. For the sake of analysis, I will separate el desmadre into these two types—activities that are fun in and of themselves, but that may include an audience, and activities that are pure performance. I should note, however, that while these two categories may be easily distinguishable as abstract types, in reality the division is not always so clear. For example, most porra members consider fighting, in the sense of coming to blows with opposing fans, as something to be performed without entering into actual physical contact, but a few claim to genuinely look forward to it.

It is in this sense of defying or mocking social norms that el desmadre is compatible with the porra members' critical ideal vision. For example, as I suggested in the previous chapter, teasing, a tame form of el desmadre, is used before games to jolt fellow porra members out of their clientelistic mode. Furthermore, their ideal vision values actions directed toward fun and excitement as ends in themselves. Porra members place a limit on el desmadre only when it eclipses support of and love for the team. Experienced fans can easily weed out potential members who are there *sólo por el desmadre* (just for the desmadre). For example, after a Pumas loss at an away game, when a potential member tore a metal seat from its moorings and flung it over the edge of the upper deck into the stands below, Ernesto called a meeting to discuss his case before the next game. He argued that the newcomer should be expelled from the group because of his aggressive and dangerous behavior. I noticed the new member slipping away from the group at that point, and I never saw him again. The porra members agreed, but, as they explained to me later, they saw other reasons for his expulsion as well. They had already suspected that he was just there for el desmadre, which was confirmed by the manner in which he tore and flung the chair. The previous week, many of the porra members yelled threats and challenges at the opposing fans during that same game, but these acts were considered to be genuinely inspired by their anger and humiliation following the loss. They identified the newcomer's actions as, at best, an inappropriately timed performance and, at worst, an authentically destructive impulse. In either case, it occurred at a moment when he would have expressed love for the team, in the form of anger and frustration, if he were a true fan.

El Desmadre: Breaking the Rules Predictably

Desmadre that does not require an audience consists primarily of two different types of activities, each of which is fun because it defies a different version of power and authority, albeit in nonrevolutionary, prefigured ways. The first involves sexualized insults aimed at the opposing players and fans. These insults question the target's manly authority and his mother's virtue, using the very language of patriarchy to do so. The second consists of a variety of bodily motions meant to challenge the authority of patrons and disturb the docility of clients, to achieve the porra members' ideal of passionate emotional expression. The former is an example of the kind of desmadre anticipated by worried, tradition-inventing intellectuals, whereas the latter has not yet been incorporated into national myths. Throughout my research, I observed both types of activities, but the first was noticeably on the wane as the second increased in importance. In the next chapter, I attempt to explain this shift by placing it in the context of a broader process occurring within and beyond the porra at the time. Here, my objective is to describe these two types of activities, placing them within the context of the versions of power and authority that they challenge.

The first type of activity is observable before and during the game, as the person standing at el poste leads the group in chants that finish with *una mentada de madre* (a mention of the mother) such as ¡*Chinga a tu madre*! (Fuck your mother!) or ¡*Hijo de puta*! (Son of a whore!). While the porra members shout these chants in an aggressive manner, they have fun doing so as evidenced by their smiles and laughter. They also invent insults for specific situations or persons that consist of albures (sexual double entendres). For example, on one occasion the porra shouted at a Chilean player who had spoken badly of the porra to the media, *Tu esposa dice que lo único que tienes de Chile es la nacionalidad* (Your wife says that the only Chile you have is your nationality), where "Chile" refers both to the country and to a hot pepper (meaning penis). During a period when one of the

Pumas players had his head shaved, they warned specific opposing players to "watch out for *el pelón*," where "un pelón" refers both to a bald person and to a penis. By portraying the Pumas player as a penis, they masculinize him and portray him as a sexual threat to the feminized opposing player. These insults are subtler than the mentadas de madre and, because they involve creativity, they are more appreciated for their humor and for the momentary victory of wits that their delivery signifies. Both the mentadas de madre and albures are always yelled or chanted, they are never sung. While their content is immanently bodily, their delivery is primary verbal except for the arm-bending motion that accompanies the mentada de madre.

I believe that these insults are considered offensive but also funny and fun because they present a challenge to the fatherly authority and motherly virtue that constitute the basis of a long-standing patriarchal ideology. This ideology owes its recent prominence to the postrevolutionary Mexican state's efforts to unite a divided nation and to legitimate its own rule through the metaphor of the patriarchal family in which the president stands as father to the nation as family (O'Malley 1986; Carey 2005). According to historian Eric Zolov (1999:4–5):

This metaphorical family was a reflection of and in turn served to reinforce an image of the stable family unit itself. The idealized family of the postrevolutionary order was one in which the father was stern in his benevolence, the mother saintly in her maternity, and the children loyal in their obedience. Faith in the father's ultimate commitment to the progress of the family—even when that father had been corrupted by temptation and error—excused his mistakes and pardoned his sins. Undergirding this sense of pardon was the vision of the mother figure as saint and sufferer, whose moral superiority and spiritual strength acted as glue for the ultimate stability of the family—and by extension the nation (as did the Virgin of Guadalupe, Mexico's semiofficial patron saint).

A mentada de madre questions the virtue of the target's mother and thus the ability of the target's father to assure her virtue and his own authority. In turn, the insult throws doubt both upon the target's own ability to protect his mother and his overall social standing as legitimate child and member of a full-fledged family. Such an insult ignores the respect men are supposed to have for the patriarchal authority of other men, thereby provoking their ire and possible vengeance. To mention the mother is to mention the unspeakable, because the mother's virtue stands for the patriarchal order that constitutes stability at the familial and societal levels. The seriousness of the insult is what makes it fun and exciting. It is important to remember, however, that this seriousness hardly makes it a revolutionary challenge to the social order. The insult questions the patriarchal order of a particular family and not patriarchy itself. In fact, the insults only make sense in the context of patriarchy, where mothers are virtuous and fathers protect them. The insults are thus prefigured or ritualized and exemplary of the small private revolution expected of young men in crisis. As such they are tolerable for everyone except for the target himself. The connection between this type of desmadre and national myths was made apparent when I asked the porra members what aspect of their practices they consider particularly Mexican, and they consistently made reference to these ritualized mentadas de madre and in particular los albures.

The other type of desmadre that does not require an audience involves a variety of bodily motions, all of which defy the manner in which fans are supposed to occupy space within the stadium. To begin with, porra members spend the whole game standing on the cement benches that are meant to serve as seats. During certain chants and songs they either jump up and down or place their arms around the shoulder of the person beside them and sway from side to side. The jumping or swaying may build in excitement until they are knocking or pushing each other off the benches and into the rows above or below them, producing a sort of chain reaction. When the Pumas score a goal, the bodily movements reach a climax as the porra members jump up and down and pile on top of one another in celebration, often ending up a few rows away from where they started. After participating in and observing such celebrations, it always seemed to me a miracle that no one had sustained a serious injury among the flying bodies and concrete benches.

While Ernesto encourages and even participates in the first type of activity, he attempts to limit the second, claiming that the team management says it will stop providing free tickets if they do not stop. He says that management argues that this roughhousing places other fans, in particular women and children, in danger and thus discourages them from coming to the stadium, causing a loss of ticket sales for the team. At times Ernesto claims that he only shares the team's concern because of the free tickets, while at others he appears to share the idea that the porra members are responsible for the safety of women and children in the stadium. Although Ernesto frames his opposition to these activities in a patriarchal family idiom, I believe that it is not a challenge to a patriarchal family order that makes these activities desmadre for the young fans. Rather, the porra members contrast these activities to the sedentary cheering of other fans and even to the sedentary nature of their own cheering involving chants, mentadas de madre, and albures. They see these cheering styles and the norms regarding how space should be used within the stadium as manifestations of the docility that accompanies clientelism.[3] Although clientelism is frequently associated with patriarchy (e.g., the metaphor of the revolutionary Mexican family mentioned above), as described in chapter 2, the porra members imagine and oppose a more urban, anonymous clientelism that creates obedience more through fear than through traditional relationships and loyalties. Also recall that the porra members only critically compare a few select clients to children (as consentidos), describing the docile majority as fearfully obedient and unable to imagine being any other way. The porra members connect the desmadre constituted by las mentadas de madre together with this docile behavior because they consider it another manner of doing just what those in power expect and even want, confirming Bartra's critical argument.

They see the set of bodily movements, such as jumping up and down, as an alternative and challenge to these clientelistic practices. In this sense, this second type of desmadre also has a more serious purpose linked to the porra members' romantic ideal. Precisely because these activities are not prefigured or accepted by those in power, including Ernesto, they consider them a vehicle for emotional expression. At the same time, the challenge that the activities pose to Ernesto and others' authority makes them fun and exciting. But the fact that these activities are unimagined and thus external to Mexico's clientelistic social order is not the only reason why the porra members consider them an ideal vehicle for emotional expression. It is also important that members adopt these movements from European and South American fans whom they watch on television, usually adding their own creative touches. The porra members idealize these fans, attributing to them a love for the game and for their teams that they claim is rare in Mexico. Through the adoption of their practices, the porra members hope to achieve their level of passionate support. Some of the porra members explained to me that they hoped to one day see the whole stadium singing, swaying, and jumping up and down like in European and South American stadiums.

I should note that I use the term "idealize" because I am not convinced that these other fans' cheering styles are simply a product of their emotion expression. Rather, I imagine that these styles have their own particular histories of development and borrowing, as well as their own particular and varied meanings for fans. Comparisons of such bodily cheering styles to working-class masculinity in England (Robson 2000) and to warfare in Italy (Bromberger et al. 1993), for example, suggest that porra members may misinterpret some of what they see on television—not that such misinterpretation really matters for their purposes.

If the porra members may sometimes misinterpret what

they see on television, then Ernesto consistently misunderstands their use of these foreign practices. Following the script provided by the national invented tradition, he tries to suppress these activities as the usual desmadre gone a little too far, as a simple rebellion from patriarchal norms, which is why he reacts by reinforcing his fatherly authority. He scolds them and reminds them of their duty to protect the women and children in and near the porra's section. The porra members even play along with Ernesto's mistaken categorization to disguise their challenge to clientelism as the less threatening small private revolution depicted in the national myths. I observed, for example, that one of the most effective responses to Ernesto's scolding was for porra members to respond with a plea of *Tranquilízate, es sólo desmadre* (Calm down, it's only desmadre). This plea seems to cause Ernesto to switch from his role of angry father to one of benevolent patriarch, reminiscent of the postrevolutionary government described by Bartra (1987) and O'Malley (1986). Instead of seeing the porra members' actions as a real threat, Ernesto sees their actions as a product of failed parenting and governance and thus assumes the task of converting them into responsible men and citizens. Thus, by portraying themselves as rebellious boys in need of strict parenting, they avoid a direct confrontation with Ernesto by drawing his attention away from their more revolutionary goal of reordering the social relations of the club to better fit their notion of passionate emotional support for the team. In the next chapter, I will return to this use of el desmadre as a smokescreen, showing how the porra members employ it along with other tactics in their struggle to resist Ernesto's authority.

The porra members were not always content to settle for such conservative measures, however. I also observed how Ernesto's attempt to control this second type of desmadre began to frustrate them and to produce a current of rebellion and then later revolution within the group (see chapters 5 and 6, respectively). Despite this eventual revolutionary current, I believe that this second type of desmadre, like other forms of romanticism, remains a patterned form of opposition within the bounds of

Figure 5. The seriousness of this expression of
friendship is interrupted by an insulting finger,
another example of el desmadre.

modern society: the porra members' primary goal is to support
the team through emotional expression, they were not exactly
ready to take to the streets, and it was primarily Ernesto's mis-
management that produced this subsequent revolutionary reaction. Their attitude toward a truly revolutionary figure, Che Guevara, demonstrates this point. For a time, a few porra members
were bringing Che flags and wearing Che t-shirts to the stadium.
When I asked them if this was an act in favor of a revolution,
they laughed and answered that it was *puro desmadre* (just desmadre), revealing, I think, that they are interesting in shaking
things up for fun's sake and to achieve passionate emotional
expression, but not in deep revolutionary change.

El Desmadre as Performance

I turn now to the type of desmadre I described above as performance. I find these performances interesting in that they estab-

lish between the porra members and their audience a relationship, meant to take on a certain form in the eyes of the audience
and another from the perspective of the performers themselves.
For porra members, this difference in how performers versus
audience perceive the same actions sets them apart. Because
an audience is required, away games are ideal for these performances of el desmadre. In addition to the stadium near-filled
with opposing fans, the bus trips to games in other cities provide
an opportunity for the porra, as a group, to interact with a segment of the general public.

The porra members tailor their performance for specific
audiences because the same performance and self-portrayal will
not shock or anger all audiences. At times, they follow the script
outlined in the national myths described above, but at others they
play upon different myths and stereotypes. When the Pumas cross
the southern part of the city to the 110,000-seat Estadio Azteca
to play against América, the porra members do the former, playing the role of the young men's angry mob. Recall that América
is seen as the team of the establishment, even by its impoverished followers, and that represents the interests of the private
and public sectors' ruling classes, exemplified by Televisa and the
PRI, respectively. The porra members represent themselves as
disorderly and destructive and thus as a threat to the social order
and private property that constitute the ruling classes' strong-
holds. According to the porra members, this self-representation reproduces the media's depiction of the young Pumas fans.
Because rich Americanistas are seen as the primary producers
of the media and poor ones are considered its most faithful and
uncritical consumers, the porra members see themselves as fulfilling these opposing fans' worst fears and expectations.

To give an example of this type of performance, during
every one of my visits to the Estadio Azteca I observed at least
one moment when some of the porra members started bending
and destroying the metal stadium seats. On one occasion when
they were in the middle of this performance, the public address
announcer made the mistake of announcing that anyone caught

destroying the seats would be arrested. Instead of discouraging the behavior, the announcement confirmed the existence of an audience and more members joined in. The eruption of vandalism ended when Jorge got carried away and started happily waving a piece of seat over his head and others told him to put it down because by that point there were police approaching.

Near the end of the game, the porra traditionally bursts into a chant stating that the América fans won't leave the stadium alive. While the porra members have no real interest in killing or even maiming the América fans on their way out of the stadium, they do enjoy the fear they believe they provoke, despite the fact that they are outnumbered by their rivals. The porra members expect the América fans to part and make way for them as they descend the ramp leading out of the stadium. If anyone does not get out of the way quickly enough, a group of porra members surrounds him and quickly relieves him of any América paraphernalia he possesses, with little or no resistance. In general, I never saw the América fans confront the porra members verbally or physically. This perhaps can be explained not only by their perception of the Pumas fans as dangerous but also by their lack of organization in anything like a porra, because América fans usually attend the games individually, as families, or with small groups of friends.

When the Pumas play away games against two of the other Mexico City teams, Cruz Azul and Atlante, both known for their working-class followings, their performance changes. The angry mob performance would not be particularly shocking to these teams' working-class fans, nor would it be easy to pull off in front of an audience that likely has some experience with genuinely angry mobs or something close to it in the context of labor struggles. During these games, the porra members portray themselves as fans of what is sometimes referred to as the "thinking man's team" because of its association with the UNAM. Meanwhile, they yell chants referring to their rivals as pot-bellied *pulque* drinkers. Pulque is an inexpensive alcoholic beverage made from the maguey plant associated with, at least within the urban context, the working class and in particular with construction workers. While working-class urban residents often celebrate the drink's properties, the porra members are playing on its association with rural Mexico, recalling poverty, backwardness, and a lack of sanitation and sophistication.[4] The provocations in this case are meant not to scare their rivals but to anger them.

The performance of el desmadre during away games in other cities starts in the bus itself. During one trip, as the bus was passing through the sprawling outskirts of Mexico City on its way out of town, I observed as José Luis and a few other porra members were mentando la madre, using the standard bending of the arm motion aimed out the window to anyone and everyone in sight. Most of their targets responded in one of two ways: either they turned away, apparently trying to avoid a confrontation, or they returned the gesture. I noted that in either case, José Luis chuckled and called the person *un pendejo* (there is no literal translation, although calling someone "an idiot" or "stupid" in English conveys a similar meaning). Although the porra members' gestures provoked fear in some and anger in others, both were viewed as pendejos because they took the bait and confused performance with reality.

The traveling fans spend the bus trip between cities drinking beer, teasing each other, and composing new chants and songs. But as they enter the city where the Pumas are to play and they once again have an audience, the performance begins anew. A favorite chant at such moments goes *Ya llegó la civilización* (Civilization has arrived), which is a transformation of the *Ya llegó el desmadre* (El desmadre has arrived) that is chanted upon arrival at the Estadio Azteca. This chant, which reappears once they are seated within the stadium, plays upon the notion that Mexico City is modern and cosmopolitan in contrast to the provincial backwardness of the rest of the country (commonly referred to by Mexico City residents as *provincia*), including even the other large cities such as Guadalajara. Not surprisingly, residents of the rest of the country dislike or even hate *capi-*

talinos, not only because of their attitude of superiority but also because centuries of tribute extraction and then later policies of economic centralization have resulted in underdevelopment of the rest of the country.[5] The chant is obviously intended to provoke anger among the hosts; as if the chant were not enough, it is not uncommon for a few porra members to urinate out the window as they recite it, reminding the *provincianos*, through this masculine sexualized act, that projects to bring civilization were never more than pretexts giving Mexico City politicians and capitalists an opportunity to exploit or, in the local idiom, *chingar* (fuck) the rest of the country.

During the game, the porra members have little trouble provoking the ire of their rivals, because their performance offers to fulfill the latter's expectation of confronting and exacting revenge upon arrogant capitalinos. The porra members just have to mentar la madre to the opposing fans, who angrily respond in kind and try to challenge individual porra members to fight even though they are separated by fences dividing sections of the stadium. The porra members play along, accepting the challenges by nodding their heads and continuing their provocation. While the home fans continue to grow angrier and angrier, however, the porra members laugh over the success of their performance. By the end of the game, the home fans are pelting the porra members with ice cubes, small glass bottles, and stones, which usually fall harmlessly because of the distance. The porra members must contemplate the possibility of really having to fight their way out of the stadium or be badly beaten in the attempt, until a police escort is organized to accompany them to the bus. The need for the escort confirms the success of the performance.

It is a success, first, because their provocation created in the audience's eyes a relationship between arrogant capitalinos and angry, abused provincianos, and, second, because the rival fans are unaware that the porra members see the relationship as one between performers and audience. Fooling the audience is more than just amusing. This difference in how the situation is perceived confirms to the porra members their distinction and

superiority in terms of what I would call a type of urban sophistication rooted in self-awareness, irony, or reflexivity.[6] During
the performance, the porra members may feign the masculine
arrogance and aggression of Mexico City politicians and capitalists, but behind this lies the arrogance and aggression of the
self-perceived urban sophisticate. I believe the latter attitudes
are less gendered than the former, in the sense that they are not
imagined in gendered terms, even if men more frequently display urban sophistication in an aggressive manner.

Another particularly striking example of el desmadre
involves what I would call the performance of sexual aggression.
At some point during the Pumas' home games, a group of female
models appears on the sidelines of the field, directly below the
porra's section in the stands. These young women are always
scantily clad in outfits that bear an advertisement, usually for a
soft drink. They remain on the field about ten to fifteen minutes,
dancing like cheerleaders or simply waving to the crowd. Without fail, the porra breaks into a song of "Olé, olé, olé, olé. Sexo,
sexo," a play upon the usual "Olé, olé, olé, olé. Pumas, Pumas."
In addition, before or after this collective chant, individuals yell
out a combination of cat-calls and insults such as ¡Te amo! (I
love you!) or ¡Sucia! (Dirty!). As usual, the chant and the cat-
calls and insults are accompanied by smiles and laughter. In this
case, I understand the porra members' actions as a performance
of a supposedly typical working-class masculinity outside the
home, imagined as constituted primarily by unreflexive and
spontaneous sexual aggression. It is a performance of precisely
what the models are supposed to provoke among male fans. I
believe that the point of the performance is to frighten onlookers
and in particular female onlookers or men who are with wives or
daughters, while mocking their audience for falling for their performance of sexual aggression. Their smiles and laughter signal
to others in the group that their actions constitute a reflexive act
and not a spontaneous expression of their sexuality. While the
performance emphasizes for the audience the dangerous and
masculine nature of el desmadre, for the performers themselves

it represents a class position, once again contrasting the sophisticated reflexive urbanite with the unreflexive sexuality of the
working-class man and with other unsophisticated people who
cannot recognize a performance when they see one. Thus, their
performance is aggressive and denigrating toward women, but
not for being "dirty" as their cries would suggest, but rather for
their willingness to take on the role of "dirty" women in the context of supposedly unreflexive working-class male sexuality.

On occasions this form of el desmadre reaches an extreme
level of aggressiveness, which though still performative or playful in nature may embarrass individual porra members after the
fact. On one bus trip to an out-of-town game, while the bus was
still in Mexico City we stopped at a traffic light beside a young
woman out for a jog wearing sweat pants and a sweat shirt. It was
early Sunday morning and she was the only person on the side-
walk. Because of traffic on the cross-street, she was also forced to
stop and wait for the light to change. A couple of porra members
shouted the usual calls of ¡*Te amo*! and ¡*Puta*! (Whore), and then
before I realized what was happening practically everyone was
at the windows on that side of bus shouting cat-calls and insults
at the woman. The woman stared straight ahead, appearing to
ignore the onslaught. As usual, the cat-calls and insults were
accompanied by smiles and laughter. In this case, however, there
was no audience and the woman was doing and wearing nothing
to provoke their sexual aggression. Besides the lack of audience
or other "performers" such as cheerleaders, what seems most
exceptional about this case is the directness of the attack. Usually
the targets of the porra members' aggression are far enough away
to contend that their awareness of the aggression only exists in
the imagination of the porra members themselves. The woman
beside the bus, however, was obviously aware of the what was
occurring, even if she pretended not to be.

Ramón, a twenty-two-year-old porra member and UNAM
student, recognized that things had gone farther than usual
when I brought up the incident a few days later during an interview. Although on other occasions porra members had dis-

missed my references to their sexual aggression, stating that it is *puro cotorreo* (just joking around), this time Ramón appeared embarrassed by what had happened. When I asked him why he had participated, he explained:

> When you see a pretty woman in the street, what do you do? Whistle? No. But if I'm with the porra and I'm *echando* [creating] desmadre, I'll probably do it. What's the difference between being alone and being with the porra? If I'm with the porra I put on my *camiseta* [jersey] del desmadre [he makes a cheering sound] . . . but alone no. But it's not because of prudishness. It's that I'd be embarrassed. How would you describe el desmadre? It's like a group of guys, going out into the street, to smoke with the gang. If you're fifteen years old and alone at home you don't smoke, but with your friends you do. Yes, probably in a group you do things you wouldn't do alone.

Although I think that Ramón's reference to doing things in a group that you would not do alone requires serious consideration (see below), el desmadre is not only constituted by actions that porra members would not do alone or that they find embarrassing. Rather, I think that Ramón is trying to explain how el desmadre may lead to things one finds embarrassing after the fact.

The incident recalls a few other examples of sexual aggression in Mexico City carried out by groups of men against individual women that I have heard of, but without witnessing first hand. During the period of my fieldwork one such incident was reported in some of the major Mexico City newspapers. After the Mexican national team qualified for the second round of the Olympic soccer competition in 1996, fans converged upon the Ángel de la Independencia, a national monument near the city's center, to celebrate.[7] The newspapers reported that the euphoric fans attacked ten women, surrounding them and chanting ¡Qué bailen las muchachas! (The girls must dance!) while attempting to tear off their clothes, which they succeeded in doing in some instances. One article noted that it did not matter if the women were accompanied by men or not, and there was a photograph of a man and woman who appeared to be together, although the man was laughing and the woman wore a pained look on her face. Another example consists of stories told to me by women about finding themselves alone in the car of a subway train with several men and getting groped by every one of them who they had to pass by as they tried to get off the train.

Eric Zolov, in his study of the history of rock and roll and of the counterculture in Mexico, described a similar scene at the screening of the Elvis Presley movie "King Creole" in 1959. According to a newspaper article, the young men in the theater "dedicated themselves to destroying the seats, which they threw onto the floor below them, along with bottles, lit papers and all class of projectiles" and later "a group of females tried to leave the theater and 'were stripped of their clothing by the savages, whose pawing left them naked'" (Zolov 1999:47). A short story about the event by Mexican novelist Parménides García Saldaña mentioned that a group of men surrounded some women and, despite the fact that they were donning the same rebellious dress as the young men, demanded that they dance (Zolov 1999:48). García Saldaña described another moment during the showing when a group of men started shouting "Meat! Meat! Meat!" at some other young women and then descended upon them grabbing their breasts and backsides (Zolov 1999:48). While all of these incidents share with the porra members' attack a lack of premeditation, they seem to me even more curious because, unlike the case of the porra, they were carried out by men who were in large part strangers to each other.

I find it difficult to interpret and explain these acts of collective, playful (which is not to say harmless) sexual aggression. There is not much help to be found in the literature on men's violence toward women in Mexico, which focuses almost exclusively on wife abuse. This gap in the literature exists despite the fact that it is common to hear both women and men in Mexico City state that they fear for women who find themselves alone with a multitude of men in a public space.[8] Zolov, however, tried to explain what happened during the "King Creole" incident as an effort on the part of the men present to reinscribe, make explicit, and emphasize their "control over women's bodies" and their "role as narrators of youth rebellion" (1999:48). I read Zolov as suggesting that the men were intentionally trying to reinscribe these roles, as if they had been challenged. In the case of the porra members' attack, however, I would say that their control over women's bodies and their role as narrators of youthful desmadre were enacted with little concern over a need to reinscribe or emphasize these roles, even if their actions unintentionally ended up doing so. Although women were sometimes able to snap the male porra members out of these roles in particular instances (see below), I do not think the porra members usually had to confront a serious challenge to their general legitimacy. Their intention, I believe, was to perform something shocking, and the script was readily available.[9] In fact, two scripts were readily available for the porra members to combine into one performance: the script of disorderly young men in crisis and that of sexually aggressive men in public spaces.

To specify what preset roles the men were playing, I return to the culturally particular, historically produced notions of national public life introduced in the previous chapter. If all women are imagined to fall into either the Virgin/Mother or the Eve/Whore categories, then any women found in public must occupy the latter category because those in the former are safe at home. In the words of Marit Melhuus (1998:364): "Women are by definition 'of the house' (as men are 'of the streets')" while "'public' is associated with sexual availability." Because women in the Eve category are reduced from full personhood to whoredom, they occupy public space not as participants in public life as such nor as members of an imagined community of citizens, but rather as mere objects of men's sexuality. Meanwhile, men, even those who are strangers to each other, can imagine themselves as fellow members of a community that is constitutive of national public life.

The Virgin/Eve myth, however, focused as it is on depicting women, cannot explain why men respond as they do to the imagined presence of sexually available women. In other words, what preestablished role are men playing in these situations? I think the answer may lay in an urban Mexican notion of men as naturally aggressive and in particular as naturally sexually aggressive. By "aggressive" here, I refer not necessarily to violence but rather to the opposite of passivity. For example, when I asked male porra members why more men play soccer than women, they responded that it is an aggressive game and that because men are more aggressive than women it attracts them more. In this sense, exemplified by soccer, aggression can be playful rather than anger-driven. Sexual aggression, whether in its playful or anger-driven form, is imagined as a sort of natural default for men when they are not called upon to play specific roles such as husband, father, or brother, in which case they relate to women as protectors.

My reference to the Virgin/Eve myth and to the notion of men's natural aggressiveness is not meant to say that men in public spaces necessarily imagine themselves in this manner nor that women are necessarily excluded from public imagery: any particular myth or belief, at least in Mexico, only enjoys limited success in creating subjects in its image. It seems, however, that certain contexts—and here the celebrations surrounding the men's national soccer team come to mind as exemplary—are particularly likely to bring men together in this manner and to reduce women to sexual objects. I would even propose that the presence of a few women may catalyze men to act in this manner, by bringing to the fore their shared aggressiveness in relation to the women's imagined passivity as sexual objects. Unless I am on the wrong track here, the availability of the roles represented in the Virgin/Eve nationalist myth coupled with the belief in men's natural sexual aggressiveness can begin to explain why the playful but harmful attacks such as those described above occasionally occur.

An interaction I observed during one game suggests that if the female victim of such an aggression is able to personalize the relationship between herself and the male participants, then she may be able to disrupt it. One of the players on the opposing team was the brother of one of the female porra members. Near the beginning of the game the male porra members began a chant calling this player *cuñado* (brother-in-law), thereby implying that they were sexually involved with his sister. The joke was aimed at the player and meant to provoke a reaction of humiliation and anger, at least if he failed to recognize *el cotorreo* (the joking around) as such. The female porra member existed in the joke and interaction as a mere passive object whom the porra members had verbally removed from her brother's protection and placed in the public realm of men as a sexual object. But soon after the chant began, she shouted "¡Nooooooo!" loudly, forcefully, and angrily. The chanting porra members grew silent and embarrassed, in some cases. Her shout succeeded in reminding the male porra members of her relationships to them as a friend, a fellow porra member, or at least as a complete, particular person, thereby displacing the relationship they had momentarily created between themselves and an anonymous sexual object.

While the female porra members usually choose not to participate in the first set of activities I described as performative desmadre simply because they do not consider these activities of interest, they find the male porra members' performances of sexual aggression particularly offensive. When I asked the female porra members what they liked least about the porra, they placed the sexual insults near the top of their list. As one fan stated, "I don't like how a girl goes by and they start to say things to her." Female porra members have another reason for their displeasure with these acts of sexual aggression. A few of them explained to me that their parents believe that just by going to the soccer stadium, the atmosphere of men's sexual aggression will make them into *loquísimas* (easy women) or *marimachas* (masculine, and thus sexually aggressive women). Therefore, their desire to go to the stadium causes conflicts with their parents and at times makes it difficult for them to attend the games. The female porra members said that they tell their parents that as long as they do not let the men *faltar el respeto* (show a lack of respect) for them, there is no threat to their sexual virtue. They claim that when a man says something to them, they just ignore him and the comment does not bother them because they have self-respect. Yet, even if these verbal attacks do not threaten these young women's sexual virtue, the attacks still occur and the female porra members recognize that they are unpleasant and at times frightening.

It is important to recall, however, a point I brought up in the previous chapter regarding the women's own version of el desmadre. It is precisely because their presence in a male-dominated public space such as the stadium transgresses the boundaries of what is usually considered appropriate and safe behavior for young women that it is fun and exciting for them to attend the games. By transgressing this boundary in an unconventional manner—that is, not as loquísimas but as women who express romantic, sexual, and platonic desires for the Pumas players in respectable ways—they resist the limits of the Virgin/Eve myth.

Conclusion

In this chapter my goal has been to portray and analyze the porra members' activities that they label el desmadre. While these activities range from ritualized insults to jumping up and down in the stands to what I call performances of aggressive masculinity, they share the excitement and diversion that comes from breaking the rules, albeit in predictable manners. To understand the concept and practice of el desmadre in its fullest sense, it is necessary to go beyond the contemporary usage of the term and even these activities in themselves to an historical process of tradition invention that occurred throughout the twentieth century. During two distinct periods of social crisis and rapid change, Mexico City intellectuals invented an image of the typical urban Mexican man characterized by his angry rebelliousness. According to this invention, rather than truly threatening the social order, this rebelliousness results in harmless momentary spurts of chaos, or in the local idiom, desmadre, that reflect the supposedly disorderly state of the men's own identities. Placed in this historical context, we can begin to understand the meaning that the porra members and their audiences attach to the performance of el desmadre and, more specifically, why these performances provoke a paternalistic reaction from authorities instead of the violence and aggression that similar actions frequently provoke in other countries such as England and Argentina. I also conceptualize these practices as performances as a caution to those who would portray such practices among soccer fans and other young men in urban Mexico as evidence of real disorder and aimless rebellion. In the following chapter, I combine the data presented in this and the two previous ethnographic chapters, resituating them in the framework of a process of struggle, awakening, and change that I observed over the course of my initial eighteen months of fieldwork.

5

The Porra as a Process of Domination, Struggle, and Innovation

In the three previous chapters, I presented my ethnographic data as if the porra and its practices remained unchanged during my initial year and a half of research. I did so, as do many anthropologists, to facilitate the description of certain aspects of my informants' lives, in this case, the porra members' ideal vision for society, their practices in the stadium, and their desmadre. By abstracting and composing a typical day at the stadium from data derived from my numerous and somewhat varied stadium experiences, I was able to convey certain key aspects of what I observed. I think that much of the variation suppressed through this strategy is arbitrary and insignificant—background noise that would only distract from what is truly important. During my fieldwork, I did record at least one example of variation, however, that formed a pattern: a process of domination, struggle, awakening, and change that I was lucky enough to experience and observe, almost in its entirety.

My objective in this chapter is to depict this process, and in doing so to portray the data presented earlier in a new light. Although there is undoubtedly a real and long-standing Pumas tradition on the field and in the stands, as the porra members themselves claim, during my research much of what passes for that tradition was being created or at least refined by the members in reaction to their own experiences in the group, and in particular, their experiences related to Ernesto. Thus, the porra members were not simply following a formula passed on to them from earlier generations of fans, and what goes on in the stadium is not simply a reflection of "real life" outside. Rather, these fans were involved in a socially engaged process of discovery and innovation, constitutive of the material world. Following Carlos Vélez-Ibáñez (1983), I believe that this process conforms to a general pattern of domination, struggle, exclusion, and innovation that can be found in organizations and groups throughout urban Mexican society. The existence of this processual pattern suggests the need for caution in our research because what looks like stable organizational or group "structure" to an outside observer may in fact constitute just one moment in a process of change.

From Authoritarianism to Democracy

My narrative begins just months before I began my research in mid-1995, when Javier, a man in his late thirties and the porra's leader since he helped to found it seven years before, left the group and stopped coming to the stadium. Porra members remember him as a sort of benevolent dictator, charismatic and witty, who filled all leadership roles and made all the decisions for the group. For example, Javier was the liaison to the team management, he took charge of the porra's internal organization, and he selected and led the cheers in the stadium. He also single-handedly decided who did and did not belong to the group and who would receive one of the free tickets he obtained from the team. They recall that Javier determined their actions through *el dedazo* (the finger pointing), an expression commonly used to describe the authoritarian top-down decision-making process frequently found in Mexican organizations. He was also remembered for his charismatic leadership and for his creativity and wit in inventing cheers. They add that not one of them even thought to question his leadership, let alone oppose him openly. Javier left the group after he received death threats from *unos porros* (some instigators) who apparently wanted to take over the group and use it for their own purposes.

Before continuing to tell Javier's story, I would like to elaborate on what a porro is and the role that the idea of the porro currently plays in Mexico City, because this will reappear in another form later in my narrative. Out of the student porras that supported the UNAM's and the National Polytechnic Institute's American football teams, there emerged in the 1960s groups of young men available to be clandestinely hired by politicians or other political actors to discredit political rivals or to mix in with and then discredit or take over student movements (Lomnitz 2005). These young men, usually from poor neighborhoods, were registered at high schools and universities, but only as a cover and to gain access to student movements. During the late 1960s and early 1970s, these groups played a significant role in helping the government to violently suppress student movements (Lomnitz 2005). Because of their original emergence from porras, these instigators are known as porros, which is precisely why the Porra Plus's members do not refer to themselves using this term.

Porro activity is less frequent and less violent now than in the 1960s and 1970s, although it does still exist. In any case, the possibility of its existence is enough to cause Mexico City residents to imagine any improper behavior among university students to be the work of porros. In this sense, the porro belongs to the same family of concepts as the mafia (see chapter 2), because both paint an image of a secretive, hierarchical, and coercive social world behind a façade of legitimacy. Specifically, a gang of porros is sometimes imagined as one tactical arm of a larger mafia, with the same pyramidical organization of patron-client relations. In contrast to earlier times when knowledge about porros was not so widespread, now such speculations can serve to exonerate "real" students and confirm suspicions that the government and businessmen frequently use underhanded practices to achieve their goals. At times the porros remain unidentified and unidentifiable, while at others the accusations serve to place blame upon and delegitimate certain parties or leaders by revealing them as dishonest and self-serving.

There continues to exist some association between las porras (cheering groups) and los porros (instigators). For example, when the newspapers accuse, usually falsely, the porra of provoking violence in the stadium, they refer to the group members as porros, suggesting that they are not real fans. For the porra members, however, there is no association beyond the linguistic: they form a porra, but are not porros in the current sense of the term. While many of the younger members playfully make this mistaken identity into part of their performed desmadre (see chapter 4), the older members try to clear the porra's name by insisting, sometimes in newspaper interviews, that they are not porros.

Under the leadership of Javier, the porros likely assumed, because of the historical link between porras and porros, that the Porra Plus was already functioning as such a gang or at least that the porra members were the kind of people who usually form such gangs: young men on the economic margins of the university community with nothing better to do and looking for some money and excitement. Although the porros would surely have caught the attention of a few members, the majority resisted the takeover, insisting on their interest in supporting the team. Soon the porros gave up and left.

A few months later, I observed as Javier tried to reclaim his old post. The recently elected president, Ernesto, asked him to leave, arguing that Javier no longer had a right to lead the group or even sit with it because he had betrayed it by abandoning it during a time of crisis. Javier tried to lead a few cheers to bypass Ernesto and appeal directly to the group members. While a few members expressed excitement over his return and followed his lead, many others ignored him or even expressed their disapproval either for the same reason as Ernesto or for another reason, which I will outline below. The opposition was enough for Javier to give up his attempt after this first try, and I never saw him again.

After Javier had left the group and the porros had given up their takeover attempt, Ernesto became the porra's first elected president. Drawing on the wave of democratic rhetoric sweeping the country, he called for an election to choose a president for the group and for meetings to reach decisions collectively. Ernesto won the election. Although, as we shall see, the porra members became disillusioned with Ernesto's reforms, they also pointed out that his leadership style was definitely distinct from Javier's. They noted that he asked them to express their opinions during meetings, even if he rarely followed through on his promises to take them into account, and he at least partially depersonalized his decision-making; for example, if they showed up early to the games, he would give them a free ticket, regardless of his personal opinion of them. With the dedazo relatively absent, the porra members began to develop an idea of themselves as potentially active participants in the shaping of the group and to form their vision of how they wanted the group to be. They began to see Javier as more authoritarian and egomaniacal than benevolent, and they realized that his leadership had stifled their creativity. Yet, while porra members admitted that Ernesto's leadership style made possible the creativity and the critical perspective they never thought to develop under Javier, they soon began to direct their newly formed criticism toward Ernesto himself, his democratic rationality, and the corruption they claimed that his democracy served to obscure.

The Emergence of "La Rebel Plus"

A couple months after I started my fieldwork, Gerardo pointed out to me a general pattern in the seating arrangement within the porra's section: those to the left of el poste tended to be UNAM students, while those to the right were more *popular* (roughly, working class). While at first I only observed a homogeneous group of young men, after having this pointed out, I began to distinguish two different styles related to physical appearance. Those whom Gerardo identified as students usually wore their hair long and often donned expensive authentic Pumas jerseys or even more costly jerseys and scarves bearing the emblems of Argentine, Brazilian, and European teams. They also wore hiking-style shoes or boots made by Nike. This style could be termed cosmopolitan because it consciously borrows from youth cultures in other urban centers around the world. Meanwhile, the working-class members wore their hair neither long nor short, used inexpensive t-shirts made especially for the porra or provided free by Nike, and wore white Nike running shoes or the black leather shoes common throughout the city. I should mention, however, that the porra, either in terms of seating arrangement or physical appearance, was never divided into two clearly distinguishable halves. There was a core of only about ten members, including Gerardo himself, who clearly and consistently demonstrated this "student" style. Meanwhile, several fans who sat near this subgroup partly shared its style of dress and got along well with its members without really being part of it.

What distinguished those members who sat to the left of el poste was not in reality their status as students—some of them were not UNAM students and many of those counted as working class were. "Working class" or even the local term "popular" is always problematic in Mexico City, where small-business owners living in supposedly impoverished areas of the city are often wealthier than university graduates and professionals and where middle-class and working-class styles may overlap and borrow from each other. Despite the problems with these labels as objective descriptions, I think that the label "student" would have made sense to many Mexico City residents because this style of dress is associated with the UNAM student body even though a walk through the campus suggests that the association is more a stereotype than a reality. In addition, by referring to themselves as "students," the members of the subgroup gained access to a discourse I heard used by porra members to authenticate their fandom. In this discourse (which is distinguishable from but overlaps with the one invoking youthful romanticism described in chapter 2), love for the team is equated to love for and loyalty to the university, which in turn, is supposedly provoked solely by the experience of studying there. In the version of the discourse used by young porra members, the UNAM is associated with its history of social critique and action in the form of student protests and Marxist-influenced scholarship. In the version used by the older and more conservative porra members, the university is lauded for the manner in which it inculcates a series of what I call patriarchal values including a respect for authority and for order. The inculcation of these values at the individual level is seen as integral to the achievement of progress at the societal level. In this second version, actors revere and thank the UNAM for its role in their lives, treating the institution itself as a sort of benevolent paternal figure. In contrast, in the first version it is depersonalized and portrayed more as a means to an end.

Ironically, both types of actors' interested claims of links to the university invoke the image of the disinterested *universitario*, concerned not with his own status, like his nemesis the Americanista, but rather with the well-being—in either socialist or patriarchal terms—of the country as a whole.[1] When the more working-class fans told me about their fandom, they would often mentioned their desire to study at the UNAM: an attempt to deflect accusations of inauthenticity or even of being porros by actual UNAM students and graduates. However, I think that this discourse was less meaningful than in the past when both the team's players and its fans were almost exclusively UNAM students. I noted that three or four middle-aged porra members were the only ones who spoke consistently in these terms.[2] If class and educational status do not explain membership in this subgroup with its distinct style of dress, I am also reticent to attribute it to residence in certain parts of the city. While nearly all of the members of this subgroup lived in the southern quarter of the city, so did many of the others thrown together as working class, often in the same neighborhoods. Thus, without providing a definitive explanation, I simply wish to suggest that what distinguished them was the style in itself and the fact that they formed a united subgroup and saw themselves as different from the rest.

I should add, however, that they were also distinguishable in the superior deployment of the youthful romantic discourse used to describe the team and their fandom. In fact, the rest of the porra often appeared to be imitating them in their own use of this discourse. The members of the subgroup also distinguished themselves through a name, "La Rebel Plus." When I asked Gerardo why they chose this English word, he explained that the Spanish equivalent, *rebelde*, with its three syllables was too long to have any snap. When I asked them if the name was meant to signal something political, they responded that it was puro desmadre, a performance of rebelliousness.

During the games, while most of the porra members talked quietly to those standing on either side of them about the game, occasionally yelling an insult at the referee and following the cheers led by the person at el poste, the members of this subgroup engaged in several additional activities. They joked, teased, and roughhoused among themselves, for example, and it was among La Rebel that I first observed the performances of el desmadre that I described in the previous chapter. Although there were no explicitly named leaders, teasing often served to create informal hierarchies based on personal charisma. When members without this charisma attempted to initiate an activity, they were teased about doing or saying something foolish and silenced by others' laughter. Such teasing limited the informal direction of the subgroup to a select few. Nonmembers who attempted to join in as equals with a joke or comment were also quickly silenced through teasing. However, the members of La Rebel also targeted the nonmembers as followers. For example, to get the whole group involved in their more bodily version of supporting the team, they began initiating a chant of *Él que no brinque es puto* (He who doesn't jump is a fag), which quickly spread to almost everyone in the section, who seemed to find it fun and funny and, in any case, they did not want to be caught standing still. Such efforts to get others involved in their cheering style were the first signs of what later became an explicit objective of this subgroup's members, to have all of the Pumas fans singing in unison while jumping up and down or swaying from side to side like in European and South American stadiums.

Opposition Arises

Opposition between two clearly demarcated groups first became apparent to me on bus trips to away games, when the members of La Rebel monopolized the back of the bus, distancing themselves as much as possible from the symbolic authority of the driver.[3] The opposing group was revealed to be not the working-class porra members, as Gerardo had suggested, who were poorly represented on these costly and time-consuming trips, but rather a group composed primarily of UNAM students and graduates who could best be described as sharing Ernesto's and others' more conservative view of the porra and its activities. In this view, the porra members, while supporting the team and even blowing off some steam, should offer an example of order and *educación* (good manners) and more specifically of family values such as respect for and defense of the group's women and children. This conservative view is analogical to the patriarchal vision of the university described above, and in some instances actors conflated the two, stating that the porra members should see themselves as representatives of the UNAM to the general public. Later, many of the younger porra members began to complain that the conservative or patriarchal vision of the group was intertwined with a system of patron-client relations, a system quite compatible with, although not equivalent to, the patriarchal order.

After possessing the back of the bus, La Rebel members would begin to provocatively mark the distinction with a chant of *Él que no chupe no es un Rebel de verdad* (He who doesn't drink [literally "suck"] is not a real Rebel), accompanied by ostentatiously consuming beer or liquor. I noted that some of the porra members near the front of the bus also drank during the ride, but in an inconspicuous manner. The opposition would then take on the form of a playful banter between the halves of the bus. A core group of those seated in one half would come up with a witty insult directed at one or more persons in the other half and would then lead their half in a reciting of the insult. The insults recalled, with their playful and creative double entendres, those directed at the opposing team during games, but without the harsher mentadas de madre. The insults provoked laughter in both halves and, although they accentuated the opposition, this common participation in the same game also served to bind the two groups together. The Rebel's participation in one of the porra's usual practices indicates that, at this point in the process, the emerging subgroup was still happy to interact on Ernesto's terms.

The Outbreak of Open Conflict

These more playful confrontations soon took on a new tone, however, as Ernesto and others like him began to see the Rebel's activities as a threat to their vision of the porra. The team began the 1996–1997 season quite badly, and the members of La Rebel began to make jokes about the team and to criticize its poor play. Before the start of one game, Nike distributed to fans yellow and red cards, similar to the ones the umpires use to signal the penalization of players, to allow them to comment by holding up the cards during the game. When the Pumas continued its streak of poor play, however, the members of La Rebel ripped eyeholes in the cards and started watching the game and cheering with the cards in front of their faces. The cards took the place of paper bags and were meant to demonstrate the shame they felt because of the team's deficient performance. While constituting a serious statement, this masking was also accompanied by the usual mockery and joking of el desmadre. When the game ended and to the Rebel members' surprise, Rodolfo, the cheerleader at el poste and one of Ernesto's close friends, began shouting at them in an angry and impassioned manner. He yelled that he was not ashamed to be a Puma, win or lose, and that if they were real Pumas fans that they would cut their

hair. The latter part of his accusation provoked even more joking and laughter among the members of La Rebel, which in turn
infuriated Rodolfo even more. At that point, Ernesto intervened,
successfully taking on the role of mediator and quieting both
sides. He said that porra members could express themselves
however they wanted, referring to both their hairstyles and the
use of the masks. I think that this statement had more to do with
leadership strategy than with Ernesto's opinion regarding what
Rodolfo had said. Ernesto seemed to share Rodolfo's idea that
Pumas fandom should consist of unconditional loyalty to the
team in the same manner that a universitario should be uncon-
ditionally loyal to the university. His reaction, however, was that
of a cool-headed leader. Soon after this incident, another senior
member confided to me that he thought that Ernesto was going
too easy on the younger members, who, he said, needed the discipline and guidance of a firm paternal hand. Ernesto continued
to distance himself from this older leadership style, however,
preferring instead what I would describe as a mix of democratic
rhetoric with mild or lenient paternalism.

Later, the members of La Rebel explained to me that Rodolfo,
because of his inability to think critically, had misunderstood
their statement with the masks. They said that they were not
ashamed of being Pumas fans, but rather of the current team
representing the Pumas. The members stated that they the fans
and not the players were the true and consistent representatives
of the Pumas, because the players come and go while they are
Pumas for life. As proof, they noted their continued presence
in the stadium and their continued cheering even while wearing the masks. They also stated that they expressed their shame
because of their love for the team, with the hope that this would
motivate the players or the management to improve.

This conflict surrounding the fans' reactions to the team's
poor performance continued and then even the players became
involved. They and the coach asked for a meeting with the porra
in an effort to put an end to the latter's criticism. The members of
La Rebel saw the meeting as an illegitimate attempt by the team

to control their actions, instead of just playing how they should on the field. Most did not attend. Those who did observed which players reacted in an accusing manner toward the fans, and then in the next game mimicked their accusations among fellow Rebel members, who then shouted in unison at the players on the field. There were also rumors that some of the players had threatened to stop donating their extra complementary tickets to the porra if its members did not change their attitude toward the team, to which the Rebel members stated that they would rather buy their own tickets than follow anyone's orders.

Just as the Rebel members were becoming aware of the implications of their dependence on others, such as their dependence on players for free tickets, Ernesto was becoming more and more embroiled in such relationships with the team management and even with Nike, one of the team's major sponsors. Both to me during an interview and to the group as a whole, Ernesto proudly stated how he had negotiated with the team management for more complementary tickets and for buses to take the group to certain away games. His bargaining chip was the collective presence of the porra. Aside from whatever effect the porra might actually have on the team's play, the team management recognized that the group helped create the atmosphere of active, passionate cheering that drew so many other fans, in particular young fans, to the stadium. However, in exchange for the free tickets and buses, the management expected something beyond the porra's ticket-selling potential.

In his postgame discourses, Ernesto began to request that the group members refrain from roughhousing and foul language during the game. He explained that the team had threatened to reverse the important gains he had obtained if they did not stop these activities, which, it believed, was scaring away many fans, in particular women and children, leading to reduced ticket sales. When his simple requests did not work, he began scolding them, stating, for example, his disappointment in their behavior. Ernesto said that he expected them to act as men should, protecting the women and children of the group from external threats, instead of doing things that could harm them physically and morally. The use of this discourse was at least momentarily successful. I observed how most of the young porra members silently hung their heads in shame. Who, after all, could openly question the validity of this notion of paternal manliness?

Once Ernesto finished, however, the effects of his speech did not last long. Not only did the porra members, and in particular those of La Rebel, return to their desmadre during the postgame activities in the parking lot and at the next game, they also began to explicitly express their dissatisfaction with Ernesto's leadership and with the agreements he had made with the team without their consent. José Luis, an eighteen-year-old porra member studying at one of the UNAM's high schools, explained to me, "I don't even get scolded at home any more, why should I have to get it from Ernesto? Youth are supposed to be desmadrosos, right?"

As Ernesto got wind of their dissent, I believe he was sincere in his confusion. He told me in an interview that he did not understand the members' dissatisfaction with his leadership because he had, in fact, achieved a lot for the group. He thought that he was truly doing them a favor by teaching and imploring them to act as men should, in contrast to typical authorities, who would just treat them as children. During an interview, José Luis tried to explain Ernesto's misunderstanding of what they were after in a manner that even the anthropologist might understand. He asked me if I would like a foreigner to be the president of my country. I could see the answer he was expecting, so I answered that I would not. He said, "Well, then you understand why we don't want an old guy like Ernesto as president of the porra." José Luis explained that because he is not young, Ernesto does not share or even understand what they want. On other occasions as well I heard porra members express their dissatisfaction with Ernesto in similar impersonal terms: he was not a bad person, in fact he meant well, but as an older man he simply could not understand them and their wants. While the porra members required the space opened up by Ernesto's democratic reforms and his lenient paternalism to come to a clear understanding of what they wanted, these innovations were not ends in themselves for the majority, especially those of La Rebel. As I have explained in previous chapters, their objectives were to freely express their heartfelt love for the team and echar desmadre.

Resistance to Commodification

During this period, along with the wave of democratic rhetoric that was sweeping the country came a flood of increasing commodification, in part provoked by the ratification of NAFTA just a couple of years before. Just as Ernesto did not invent or even introduce the democratic rhetoric that he espoused, he was not individually responsible for the increasing commodification of the team and the fans that was occurring simultaneously. When I began my research, the porra members noted that the Pumas team was unique in the league not only for its philosophy of puros jóvenes, but also because of its distinctive form of ownership. They explained that the Pumas is the only team in the league owned by a not-for-profit corporation, which directs all profits back to the team or to the UNAM, while the alumni on the board of directors absorb any financial losses. They suggested that this form of ownership protects the team from the forces and logic of the market, allowing it to maintain the practice of only youths, even if this were not the most profitable strategy. As evidence of this distance from the market, they noted that the Pumas was the only team without the name of a sponsor on their uniform and without advertising on the pitch.

During my research, however, this distance began to shrink rapidly. A strip of rotating advertising signs were added to the side of the field and the names of corporate sponsor appeared on the players' jerseys and various other places around the stadium. The most visible sponsor was Nike, which began an intensive advertising campaign. Nike representatives appeared during half time to sling or kick t-shirts and balls into the stands.

They set up displays of Nike products in the parking lot together with free games, such as kicking a ball through a target, for which winners were awarded Nike products and all participants received key-chains and other trinkets with the Nike logo. They also distributed posters and collectors' cards with the best and best-looking Pumas players sporting Nike products, thereby commodifying another aspect of their youthfulness. These were most popular among female fans, whose valorization of players' youth was somewhat different from the male fans, because it took into account the personalities and physical attractiveness of specific players both on and off the field.

Nike's onslaught was also directed at the porra as a group. Besides the players, the porra members were the most visible human presence at the games, both for the spectators in the stadium and for television viewers because the broadcasts occasionally included shots of the porra in action. This visibility gave the group advertising potential. Through Ernesto, the company attempted to establish itself as the group's sponsor. They gave him trinkets and painters hats with the Nike swoosh and the Pumas logo to distribute to the porra members. Then it provided him with t-shirts and a banner to hang over the wall of the upper deck in front of the group, made especially for the porra. At first, porra members were happy to receive the trinkets and t-shirts. I think that Nike's newness both in Mexico and in soccer gave it a youthful feel that appealed to them in contrast to more established brands. A look around the stadium at that time revealed most fans wearing Nike sneakers or hiking boots and many with Nike hats or t-shirts. In addition, porra members were never first and foremost anti-market, but rather pro–emotional expression.

The first complaints I heard about Nike were related to clientelism and corruption. They protested that Ernesto was giving more of the paraphernalia to his clients rather than distributing it evenly and openly, and some even claimed that he was receiving financial compensation from Nike when it was really the whole group that should be rewarded for its advertising potential. Héctor, for example, noted that he did not mind if Ernesto made the porra into a business, but that it should be "Fifty, fifty,"[4] meaning that the earnings should be distributed equally. The members of La Rebel, however, soon led the group in another form of dissent when they began to feel that Nike's sponsorship was affecting their passionate support of the team in concrete ways. This began when Ernesto informed them that one of the conditions of receiving the Nike t-shirts was that they all wear the shirts to every game. He added that the uniformity would create a superior collective appearance analogous to coordinated cheering. After hearing this, the members of La Rebel as well as others refused to wear them at all, often returning to their store-bought Nike-made jerseys, because this obligation contradicted their pure expression of love of the team. Now conscious that such commercialization could affect their most valued practices and beliefs, other critiques emerged. Many complained that the Nike swooshes on the t-shirts, banner, and hats were bigger and more visible than the Pumas logos. They commented sarcastically that they felt like they were supporting Nike rather than the Pumas.

Their dissatisfaction with this entanglement with Nike first produced an act of resistance during one game when Nike apparently pushed its essentially free advertisers too far. The following excerpt from my field notes recounts how events unfolded that day:

When we arrived at our seats in the stadium, there was a giant Pumas *playera* [jersey] laid out on the center of the field. It was white with blue trim and with a gold puma's head in the middle. On the rear inside part of the collar there was a Nike tag as on a real shirt, but the jersey did not say Nike or have a swoosh anywhere else. Just before the game when a few porra members went down to the field to do the usual flag waving during the introductions, instead of holding flags, some of them gathered around the edges of the jersey. They lifted it up and waved it by moving its edges up and down. It became apparent that it was only one layer of nylon and not like a real jersey that a giant could actually wear. There were different reactions to the shirt among the members in the stands. I heard José Luis and some others say ¡*Es chingón*! [It's cool!]. A couple of members hissed at it to show their disapproval.

When the porra members on the field returned to the stands, they brought the shirt with them. Starting down near el poste, the porra members laid it out over their heads, so that it covered about twenty-five people, and began to slowly pass it upward through the section. Previously, I had seen the porra members do the same with their large banners, the idea being to create an interesting effect for those in other parts of the stadium. They would see the giant banner, displaying perhaps the Pumas logo and "Porra Plus," moving through the stands apparently by its own mysterious force. The porra members also enjoyed the strange feeling of being covered by the large piece of cloth.

As the giant jersey began to move toward me, I noticed that someone had taken out a pair of scissors. When the shirt passed over the head of the scissors bearer he cut up the part of the shirt that was above him. Those standing near him laughed with approval and pulled out pocketknives to join in this act of diversion and opposition. About a quarter of the jersey ended up shredded. After that game, we never saw the jersey or anything like it from Nike again.

After the game and building on the momentum created by the giant jersey, a group of porra members made a collection and gathered volunteers to sew and paint a banner without the Nike swoosh to hang in front of the group, replacing the one Nike had provided. At the following game, they hung it so as to cover the Nike logo on the other banner. When Ernesto saw this he reprimanded them and had it removed, suggesting to them that he cared more for his relationship to Nike than for supporting the team.

Ernesto reacted to this dissent by trying to convince the porra members that what he was doing was for the benefit of the porra. This attitude, however, just confirmed to the more skeptical young members, and especially the Rebel members, that he embodied the clientelistic subjectivity that they were growing more critical of every week, because he was letting the team's and Nike's demands rather than his love for the Pumas guide his actions. They realized that, at best, Ernesto was on a different wavelength and, at worst, his efforts to help the group were only a mask for his own financial interest.

Meanwhile, the more critical porra members also began to comment on how Ernesto was using his control over the distribution of these benefits to create clientelistic ties to the porra members themselves. They noted that his threats that the team and Nike would cut off the flow of free tickets and paraphernalia did in fact serve to elicit attitudes of obedience from many porra members. The most obedient members were generally those who were already less likely to engage in the new cheering practices introduced by La Rebel, so it could be said that Ernesto's threats did not have much of an effect. The members of La Rebel, however, now saw not just Ernesto but also his obedient clients as impediments to their objective of truly Puma-izing the group's cheering because the obedient clients marked the limits of their influence. They began to counter Ernesto's benevolent giving and his threats with their own mockery and teasing. Thus, before the games when Ernesto announced that he was going to start distributing the free tickets and most of the porra members rushed to gather around him, some Rebel members starting making sheep sounds or imitating chants used in political protests, which are commonly interpreted as shows of loyalty to union or other organizational leaders rather than genuine expressions of opposition. In the stadium, when Ernesto was distributing Nike trinkets (of which there were usually not enough to go around) by throwing them to individual members, La Rebel again raised its mocking, critical voice. To attract Ernesto's attention and elicit a trinket, some porra members would cry out to him in a pleading tone.

The Rebel members imitated this tone and stated things like "Ernesto, kick me in the face, please," thereby suggesting that the pleaders were willing to belittle themselves before Ernesto to receive just about anything. I would add that the statement also implies they are acting like clients, concerned with showing their interest in what the patron has to give and seeking the patron's acknowledgment of their status as clients. While the effect of the Rebel's mockery was far from complete, it did serve to limit some porra members' subservience to Ernesto and also to sensitize others to this critical perspective.

Ernesto's Response: Co-optation and Emasculation

Up to this point, Ernesto appeared to see the members of La Rebel and their actions as no more than a minor disturbance of his vision of the porra. He imagined them much as they presented themselves, as jóvenes desmadrosos (disorderly youths) conducting "small private revolutions" (Bartra 1987:162) and requiring nothing more than a bit of fatherly guidance to keep them under control. But as the members of La Rebel became increasingly critical of his efforts to control their actions and of his growing dependence on the team management and Nike, he started to see them as a potential threat not only to his vision of the porra but to his leadership. He responded to this threat in two ways. First, he worked to draw key porra members, the leaders among their peers, into his fold, a common process in Mexican society and politics often referred to as co-optation. This drawing in of leaders quells resistance either by provoking others to follow suit or further disempowering them if they choose not to join. Carlos Vélez-Ibáñez (1983) described this process as "rituals of marginality" in reference to the majority who both lose their leaders and remain excluded. Second, and with the help of his co-opted allies, Ernesto attacked the Rebel members, painting them as the porra's weak, unmanly link to discredit them among the rest of the group.

The material benefits that Ernesto had obtained in his nego-
tiations with the team management and Nike became his principal medium of exchange in his attempts at co-optation. I began
to notice, for example, that his distribution of Nike paraphernalia was biased toward the porra members with the most influence over their peers. Also, when the team provided without
charge a bus for a trip to an away game or once when a television program invited the porra to make an appearance, Ernesto
first contacted these key members, leaving only a few places for
the rest of the group. His objective was to use this gifting of limited resources to evoke loyalty, or at least compliance, among
the group's informal leaders. Having achieved these leaders'
allegiance, or at least silence, the other members would either
follow or be unable to mount any sort of opposition.

None of this had to be explained to the porra members,
who were well aware of this type of leadership strategy from
various other contexts in Mexican society. In fact, they quickly
labeled Ernesto's actions *consentimiento* (favoritism, spoiling).
In chapter 2, I discussed how porra members use this concept
to describe relationships between players and management on
teams other than the Pumas. I noted how porra members claim
that management *conciente a* (spoils; shows favoritism toward)
the best players through gifts and praise to acquire their loyalty,
creating a relationship analogous to that between a parent and a
spoiled child. The porra members began to distinguish between
those who willingly entered into this kind of relationship and
those who did not, referring to the former as his *consentidos*
(favorites). They used this labeling not just to distinguish but to
discipline as well. By making explicit the existence of a relationship in complete contradiction with all that was valued among
Pumas fans, they were sometimes able to shame fellow members into rejecting all or at least some of Ernesto's advances.
Referring to one of these co-opted members as Ernesto's *picador* (the bullfighter who goads the bull by pricking it) was an
even more effective manner of implementing discipline through
shame; as explained in chapter 2, calling someone Ernesto's

picador implies that he penetrates Ernesto sexually in exchange for privileges and gifts.

Ernesto struck a powerful blow to this resistance, however, when he succeeded in co-opting the newly elected cheerleader at the post, Juan. Rodolfo, the former cheerleader, and a close friend of Ernesto, had stepped down in response to complaints from many of the younger members, and in particular those of La Rebel, who demanded someone with more energy who was able to keep the cheering going throughout the entire game. Ernesto declared an election would be held to determine who would occupy the post, and Juan's candidacy satisfied most of the members. Besides being energetic and already a leader among his peers, Juan possessed a booming voice. While the twenty-year-old Juan, who works for the city's subway system, was not a member of La Rebel, he got along well with its members and was not considered one of Ernesto's friends or consentidos. This changed, however, soon after his election.

Juan continued in Rodolfo's footsteps, following Ernesto's instructions regarding which cheers to lead. At times he willingly gave in to the Rebel's resistance and took up their songs, while at others he grew angry and tried to silence them. Because of his friendship ties with Rebel members and because of his impressive charismatic and physical presence, he had more success than Rodolfo at actually regaining control of the lead. Also, Juan's loyalty to Ernesto became an important tool for the latter during the group's meetings (see below) when Juan and his friend Rubén would stand at the front of the group on either side of Ernesto silencing most anyone who dared to speak by making fun of them and provoking laughter among the rest of the members. Other porra members noted that in exchange Juan and his friends were receiving special treatment. Neither Juan nor his closest friends had to show up early before games to add their name to the list for tickets because Ernesto always set aside tickets for them. Also, they showed up for the games already decked out in the best and newest Nike freebees.

The Rebel members pointed out that Ernesto's favoritism

involved showering praise on his consentidos in exchange for their loyalty. In particular, I was able to note how Ernesto began to praise Juan and Rubén for certain ideas that he had opposed previously. During a home game against Cruz Azul, a cross-town rival, a group of porra members decided to do a *vuelta olímpica* (a victory lap) during halftime, not on the track around the field but rather around the stadium at the level of the upper deck. Juan grabbed a Pumas flag and a group of about twenty members took off behind him. When they got to the far side of the stadium, which was filled by a large contingent of Cruz Azul fans, fighting broke out and the police intervened to break it up. After the game Ernesto began by scolding those who went, stating that such behavior would endanger the privileges provided by the team. While he spoke, Juan shook his head back and forth repeating "no, no, no." When Ernesto had finished, Juan took advantage of his position standing beside Ernesto (most everyone else was sitting in front of them) and stated that they had gone in peace and that if he is attacked he is going to defend himself. Instead of opposing or silencing Juan, as he usually did in such circumstances, Ernesto changed his tune and stated his agreement. Subsequently, Juan and Rubén insisted during meetings that conflicts with fans at away games should be dealt with by force. Whereas Ernesto had previously reprimanded porra members for any behavior that might provoke opposing fans, he now complimented Juan and Rubén on their bravery and manliness. It soon became clear that this praise was part of a strategy with two different objectives. On the one hand, it fed into the exchanges with Juan and Rubén that assured their loyalty; on the other hand, it provided Ernesto with a discourse connecting manliness, violence, and courage with which to discredit members of La Rebel.

A Change in the Rules of the Game: Manliness, Violence, and Courage

I first observed Ernesto's efforts to achieve this second objective during and after a trip the porra made to an away game in the city of Irapuato in February 1997. Unlike most trips to other cities, this one promised to be fairly uneventful because the Pumas' opposition, Atlante, is a team from Mexico City and was just using the Irapuato stadium temporarily for its home games. Most of the fans in the stadium seemed neutral, and the game passed without incident. A conflict occurred, however, as the bus was driving away from the stadium and passed through a thick crowd of pedestrians. A porra member sitting at the back of the bus and holding an Irapuato team flag he had just bought was asked by a person in the crowd outside to trade it for a Pumas flag. Before the exchange could take place, the pedestrian with the Pumas flag snatched the Irapuato flag and refused to give anything in return. In response, the rest of the porra members sitting at the back of the bus, mostly Rebel members, started mentando la madre to the perpetrator. In turn, he and his friends started throwing bottles and ice cubes at the bus.

Juan, who was sitting near the front, was the first off the bus to confront our attackers, and those at the back tried to follow. Gerardo, one of the informal leaders of La Rebel, stated solemnly to those still seated around him that we should all get off the bus to support those who had already done so. In addition to Juan, Daniel and Ernesto also made it off the bus, but the pressure from the crowd outside prevented anyone else from getting off. I could see one of our attackers taking his belt off, and Daniel's arm was struck by a bottle. It looked like we were confronting a large group, although later someone said they were really only three. When I got halfway to the front of the bus with anxious porra members packed in front of and behind me, Juan and Ernesto had gotten back on and were pushing us back toward the rear of the bus and telling everyone to take their seats. Once the bus got moving, Juan went to the back of the bus and started scolding everyone there for having started the conflict, and he refused to listen to how it had all started with the theft of the flag.

At a postgame meeting a couple of weeks later, Ernesto brought up the incident. He used it to contrast his and Juan's bravery with the cowardice of the Rebel members, who he said had started the conflict but had then stayed on the bus, leaving him and Juan alone outside. This version had little to do with what had actually happened that day, but there were only a handful of people at the meeting who had been sitting at the back of the bus and who knew what Ernesto was doing. Because of Ernesto's effective control over the meetings (see below), none of them dared question him there. They did, however, express their frustration over Ernesto's actions among themselves; the incident made it clear to them and others who were already critical of Ernesto's leadership that a battle had begun.

A similar situation arose a couple of months later as the Pumas faced the team from Ciudad Nezahualcóyotl (Neza) in the first round of the eight-team playoffs. The winner was to be decided by a home-and-away series with the first game at the Pumas' home stadium and the second one, a couple of days later, in Neza.

To understand some of the events that I am about to describe, it is important to say a few words about Ciudad Neza and how it is viewed by many Mexico City residents. Ciudad Neza, located just east of the city on the dry Texcoco lakebed, was settled starting in the 1960s as urban housing failed to accommodate the influx of migrants from the countryside. Prior to settlement, the dry lakebed was federal land, supposedly unplanned and unfit for housing due to the propensity for flooding and the lack of urban services. Despite the legal and environmental obstacles, however, thousands of families laid claim to plots and built houses. Eventually, either through individual or collective struggle, most residents legalized their claims and successfully pressured the government to install urban services. By the 1980s, the settlement had over a million people and was the third most populated city in Mexico. Jokingly referred to as "Neza York," it had the reputation among capitalinos of being a violent and dangerous place, ridden with crime and controlled by gangs. Here I am concerned less with whether or not this reputation was deserved than with the fact that it existed, including among porra members.

The porra members do not view the Neza team as a significant rival, by which I refer not to its potential to compete on the field, but rather that it does not represent anything against which the Pumas followers define their own fandom. Because it was the playoffs, however, hopes and tensions were high. On the day of the first game, a bus filled with Neza fans passed close by the area of the parking lot where the porra members gather before games. The porra members and those on the bus exchanged insults, and someone on the bus threw an orange peel at the porra. As a second bus approached, the porra members armed themselves with trash and rocks, which they threw at the bus without significant effect. This was the first time I had observed such a confrontation at the stadium, and I think it can be explained by the fact that it was a playoff game, but mostly because it was rare for opposing fans to arrive together in a bus and to pass by that area of the parking lot.

During the first half of the game there was more than the usual friction between La Rebel and Juan at the post. This heightened friction could have been due to the tensions created by the playoff situation or the skirmish with Neza fans before the game. It seemed to me at the time that there was tension simply because it was a night game and it was raining. Also, before the game Ernesto had once again relayed a message from the team management that they did not want the porra members to jump up and down during games. This time, however, it was because the stadium supposedly was not in sufficiently good condition to withstand it. When he first said this, the porra members had bowed their heads like reprimanded children. But once the porra was inside, the jumping, led by La Rebel, continued as usual. Although Ernesto said nothing, Juan kept yelling at the rest of the group to be seated. The members of La Rebel ignored him or perhaps intensified their jumping because of his protests. Among the rest of the group, some followed La Rebel and others obeyed Juan.

The tensions heightened even further when Ernesto handed a bunch of flyers to Gerardo, asking him to pass them back toward the part of the stands above the porra's section. The fly-ers stated that the porra was inviting all Pumas fans to attend the next game in Ciudad Neza and that they should be at the Puebla metro stop at a particular time on the day of the game. When he read the flyer, Gerardo started shouting at Ernesto, saying that the porra wasn't just his and that he wasn't going to be happy until it was. He said the group should be called the "Porra Ernesto." He also called him *Javier Dos* (Javier II), referring to the group's former leader and the complete control over the group that he exercised. Gerardo's reaction, which took Ernesto off guard, was nonetheless congruent with one of the porra members' main complaints about his leadership. Accord-ing to Gerardo, the word "invite" implied that the porra was going to pay for other fans' trip to Neza and even supply them with tickets.

Besides the potential for confusion and conflict that this could cause, I think that what most bothered Gerardo was that Ernesto thought he could speak for the porra, despite his basic misunderstandings of what was most important to the majority of young members. In this case, Gerardo seemed to be reacting to Ernesto's notion that just anyone could show up and sit with the porra in contrast to his and others' idea that membership was restricted to those who had proven their love for the team. After he finished shouting, Gerardo continued his critique by changing the words of the cheers into insults aimed at Ernesto. For example, instead of singing "If you support the Pumas, clap your hands," he sang instead "If you don't like Ernesto, clap your hands." Several porra members joined him, especially those of La Rebel. It is important to note that the conflict between Gerardo and Ernesto had been building for some time. Not only was Gerardo the informal leader of La Rebel and its most outspoken member, he had also consistently resisted and even rejected Ernesto's many and concerted attempts to win him over and convert him into a consentido.

By halftime the Pumas were losing 2–0, a situation that did nothing to alleviate the already-building tensions. In fact, the tensions began to spread beyond the conflict between Ernesto and La Rebel to include other actors within and beyond the porra. As the fans' disappointment grew, their support started to die out. In response, Juan began shouting from the post that they had to support the team in bad as well as good times. His urging inspired a few porra members, but when he directed it at the fans above the group's section, I noticed that one of them repeatedly gave him the mentada de madre gesture. La Rebel took up this cause on its own, chanting at the other half the porra: *Pan y vino, pan y vino, pan y vino. Él que no grite por Pumas, ¿para qué chingados vino?* (Bread and wine, bread and wine, bread and wine. If you aren't shouting for the Pumas, why the hell did you come?). In response, one of the porra members sitting on the other side yelled that he had been coming to the games and supporting the team for more than ten years and if he did not want to cheer he did not have to. The final score was 3–1 in favor of Neza, but on the way out of the stadium most of the porra members said they would go to the next game anyway, even though it would be difficult to make up the goal differential on foreign turf.

By the time I got back to the area of the parking lot where the group gathers before and after games, we noted an ambulance nearby and that its crew was treating a porra member for head wounds. Word went around that a Neza fan had hit him with a bottle, and it was not until the next day that I learned that in fact the injury had resulted from a fight with another Pumas fan. This rumor, however, combined with the confrontation that had occurred before the game, the loss, and the tensions within the porra, put the porra members on edge. So when three buses full of Neza fans again passed close by the porra's section of the parking lot, several porra members began arming themselves with stones. Gerardo, who was standing close to me, said that we should leave the area because if they all decide to get off the buses we would be outnumbered—and by angry fans from Neza of all places! At that point we started to hear the sounds of stones hitting the sides of the buses and of shattering windows.

As the buses stopped, a few fans got off and some fighting broke out. My observation was interrupted, however, by several porra members charging toward me, and I turned and ran with them. When we had reached a safe distance, I noted that those with me were almost all members of La Rebel. Gerardo said that after this the Neza fans would be waiting for us and it would be better not to go to the next game. The others present agreed. When the buses had left, we returned to the porra's section of the parking lot.

On the following day, a newspaper article stated that members of the Porra Plus had attacked buses transporting Neza's porra, causing damage to the buses and injuring one fan who had been hit in the head with a stone. It included an interview with the leader of Neza's porra, who stated that he was going to sue the Plus to cover the cost of the damages and that the Neza fans would be waiting to exact revenge at the next game. Later that day Ernesto called me and asked me to meet him and a few other porra members at the newspaper that had published the article. I thought that he would deny the involvement of the porra, but when he explained his strategy to us outside the newspaper's offices, it seemed that he wanted to show that the Neza fans were just as responsible for the fighting as the Plus. He told us that the leader of Neza's porra had contacted him about paying for the damages, but he said he wasn't worried because, as a lawyer, he was confident he could defeat them in a legal battle. The Pumas' press agent was also supposed to have come, but because he did not show, Ernesto decided it would be better not to talk to the newspaper, and we left. But before we departed, Ernesto brought up the rising dissent to his leadership among porra members and claimed that he would step down as president if that was what everyone wanted.

Two days later, the porra members assembled at the Puebla metro stop with the idea of making the short trip to Ciudad Neza as a group. As they had promised, most of the Rebel members were absent. At one point I overhead Ernesto explaining to a gathering of porra members that, in fact, it had been Gerardo's idea to include the word "invite" on the flyers and he had told him to take it out. He asked rhetorically if Gerardo had a right to get angry with Ernesto for his own mistake. Then Juan gave a sort of speech about how we should not run away during conflicts with opposing fans because showing our weakness only makes the situation worse, whereas by just holding our ground the numbers would discourage aggression. Juan praised the courage of those who had stayed and fought, and especially those who had done so despite not having been involved in the initial stone throwing. He included himself and Ernesto among those who had demonstrated appropriate behavior in this manner. Without mentioning the possibility that those who had run simply wanted to avoid the conflict, he accused them of cowardice. Although neither Ernesto nor Juan stated any names or mentioned La Rebel, it seemed fairly obvious who they were referring to and calling cowardly. (Later that day, when I talked to Gerardo on the phone, he said that someone had told him that Ernesto was spreading the rumor that La Rebel had not only run away but had initiated the attack in the first place.)

I noticed that Ernesto was consulting with Juan and other consentidos and then he approached the rest of the group to make an announcement: the porra would not go to Neza so as not to risk entering into a conflict with fans there. I heard grumbling, and then Daniel, who lived near the metro stop, suggested that everyone come to his house to watch the game on television. Ernesto accepted the invitation. About half of those present, however, ignored Ernesto's decision and started organizing the trip to Neza. A few porra members negotiated with the driver of a *pesero* (a small bus seating about twenty passengers) to take them to Neza. José Luis and Ramón convinced me to come along, and we jumped on the bus.

They asked if I was scared going to Neza, and I said that I was. When I asked them, they claimed they were not but that we should take precautions, such as taking our porra t-shirts off or wearing them under our sweaters or jackets. Ramón explained that the members of La Rebel were also scared and that's why they didn't come. I asked why some of the porra members were scared, but others were not. Ramón said that those who were scared were *burgués* (bourgeois) and had not grown up in neighborhoods like his or José Luis's, where fights and other forms of violence were daily events. I should note that Ramón and José Luis in their current activities could be considered more burgués than some of the Rebel members: Ramón was studying engineering at the UNAM and José Luis was finishing high school at one of the UNAM's *preparatorias*. The difference they were referring to had more to do with their internalization of habits and norms in relatively rough neighborhoods at a young age.

I asked if they thought Ernesto had decided not to go because he was scared. They said that he was scared of something different: bad publicity and ruining his good relations with the team and with Nike. Then José Luis and Ramón began expressing their frustration with Ernesto's leadership. They stated that he had no right to decide that the porra should not go to Neza. If individual people did not want to go, that was fine, but no one, and especially not *un ruco* (a colloquial term for an old man, a geezer) who doesn't understand the young fans, should decide for the whole group. I should add that while not members of La Rebel, Ramón and José Luis both got along well with its members and shared a lot of their critical feelings toward Ernesto and his leadership. It is conceivable that aspects of their critical perspective were picked up from the Rebel members, who were the first to openly express this dissatisfaction, but I cannot confirm whether this is actually the case.

José Luis and Ramón told me that Ernesto had called a meeting on the following Saturday to address complaints over his leadership. Ramón said that he was going to organize another meeting the day before with La Rebel to discuss strategy. He said it was important to have a united front against Ernesto at the general meeting because most of the porra members were *borregos* (sheep) and, even if they agreed with their criticism of Ernesto, they would follow him at the meeting. José Luis added that this was especially true of the new members, who did not yet fully understand what being a porra member and a Puma fan was all about. While a sort of intellectual in the context of the porra, Ramón did not have the charisma to be a leader and realized that alone, without the collective force of La Rebel and especially Gerardo's leadership, he would be lost.

Ramón outlined his proposal to Jóse Luis and me. He said that Juan should be removed from the post because he's not creative enough and he's too deep in Ernesto's pocket. He said that three porra members should rotate at the post so they do not get tired. He also proposed that Samuel, one of only a couple of porra members older than Ernesto, should handle all the money, keeping it out of Ernesto's hands. Unlike Gerardo, Ramón was not so ambitious as to propose removing Ernesto from power completely, but he said that if Ernesto kept angering the porra members he would eventually lose his power. I asked if Ramón thought these proposals should be voted on at the meeting and he said no, that a vote would go Ernesto's way because the majority of the porra members are either too new to understand the issues or too sheepish to oppose Ernesto. Ramón said that it would be better for small groups of members to reach a consensus among themselves and then to reach a consensus among the groups at the meeting. While this idea sounded like a good way in theory to counter Ernesto's divide and rule tactics (see below), I thought at the time that it would be difficult to put into practice. Besides La Rebel, such smaller groups did not really exist, and even La Rebel was not organized so as to act as a collective block in a formal setting such as the porra's meetings.

When we got to Neza, everyone agreed it would be better to split up into groups of two or three to enter the stadium, so as not to attract too much attention. Once inside everyone converged on the area reserved for visiting fans, and I was surprised to find other Porra Plus members, already outfitted with Pumas clothing and reassembled for cheering, with El Caco, a twenty-two-year-old porra member rumored to be a thief and drug dealer,[5] leading the cheers. Neza's porra was not nearby and was thus not an immediate threat. But the fans around our section tried to intimidate us and made signs meant to suggest that we were frightened. They also threw some cups, bottles, and other trash at us and sent firecrackers jetting our way. I noticed that the porra members around me did not seem too concerned, even when a woman a few rows away was burned by a firecracker. One porra member even fell asleep for a moment at halftime, claiming he was hung-over.

El Caco was particularly impressive. Despite being completely exposed to the opposing fans aggression because he was standing on a small wall in front of our section, he joked casually with the Neza fans and ignored the firecrackers whizzing by him. His fearlessness and confidence seemed to be his best defense, in fact, evoking respect from the Neza fans around us. The porra also used this same strategy collectively. At moments during the game when the verbal and physical attacks on us built—for example, when the Neza team scored goals, which it did several times that day—Ramón suggested to El Caco to tell everyone to stand and to lead us in La Goya, the team cheer. Our confident response to the Neza fans' aggressions was indeed effective in quieting them.

Divergence from Ernesto's thinking was manifest in the number of porra members present and in their ability to reassemble the porra so easily without any of its usual leaders. At moments, more direct opposition also surfaced. One porra member suggested to El Caco that he lead a chant saying "Ernesto, wherever you are, chinga a tu madre." El Caco refused and told him to do it himself, which he did not, provoking a general chant of *le faltan huevos* (he lacks balls). No one criticized El Caco for refusing, because it simply was not his wild, fun-loving style to make such an aggressive attack. At halftime, Ramón approached Samuel, the senior member he proposed as treasurer, and explained to him his ideas for changes in the porra. Samuel agreed, further suggesting a high level of consensus regarding dissatisfaction with Ernesto's leadership, because Samuel was perhaps even more conservative and critical of La Rebel than was Ernesto. I imagined at the time, however, and was confirmed in my thinking the following week, that much of this opposition would dissolve in Ernesto's presence as it had done it previous meetings and direct confrontations.

In this atmosphere of opposition to Ernesto's leadership, I was surprised to find some of the porra members looking to locate a replacement paternal authority figure. Ramón and José Luis, for example, approached Samuel near the end of the game and asked him to talk to the police and request that they escort us out of the stadium. This was something that Ernesto commonly did at away games to assure our safety and avoid violent conflict. Samuel, not particularly drawn to leadership, just ignored Ramón and José Luis, leaving them without a patriarchal social structure, even though the desire for one was obviously there. Even without the police escort, we left the stadium without incident. Once again the porra members took off their t-shirts and split into small groups. A couple of Neza fans yelled things at us, but we ignored them and hopped on a bus that several porra members including El Caco had already boarded. Despite the team's loss and elimination from the playoffs, El Caco led us in various cheers once the bus was at a safe distance from the concentration of Neza fans near the stadium. Individual porra members began mentando la madre to passersby now that they could again safely take the role of playful aggressors.

The Meeting

The following Saturday about fifty porra members traveled from various parts of the metropolis to the Pumas' stadium for the meeting. Ernesto arrived late, making everyone wait, perhaps to remind us that the meeting begins when he arrives, not at the appointed time. As usual, we met in one section of the stadium parking lot, with the porra members sitting or standing in a semicircle around Ernesto. Juan and Samuel stood on either side of Ernesto, bringing to my mind the roles of bodyguard and advisor, respectively. Samuel, apparently, was not going to act on his earlier agreement with Ramón's proposals for change.

Gerardo sat directly in front of Ernesto, which was by no means a coincidence.

Even before the meeting began, the two had rehashed their argument over the word "invite" on the flyers. In the past when disagreements arose between Ernesto and Gerardo, Ernesto would usually *consiente a* (spoil) him by downplaying the conflict, offering him more responsibility in the leadership of the porra, or publicly praising his actions. Other porra members had explained to me that, although Ernesto could not maintain this control over Gerardo for very long, Ernesto's special treatment made it difficult for Gerardo to continue to dissent at that moment. This time, however, Ernesto did not give in. Gerardo argued passionately; he raised his voice and became visibly agitated. As Gerardo explained to me, he was passionate when it came to these disputes with Ernesto because his motivation comes from his love for the team not out of self-interest. Ernesto, on the other hand, an experienced lawyer, remained calm. Neither of them would back down, and they stopped arguing after a few minutes. Regardless of whether this was Ernesto's intention, however, the differences between their argumentative styles gave him an advantage during the rest of the meeting. Gerardo's frustration over the argument seemed to drain him of his ability to stand up to Ernesto.

When it appeared that the argument had stopped, Ramón stood up from where he was sitting and introduced what he was about to say by stating that he had been coming to the stadium for more than eight years and that he had been a member of the porra for six of those. I often heard porra members begin speaking at meetings by making such claims, which had the purpose of demonstrating their commitment and knowledge as Pumas fans and porra members and in turn legitimating their right to speak and validating their opinions. I never saw porra members question the use of such claims to seniority, despite what seems to me to be an inconsistency with the Pumas' philosophy of "giving young people a chance." Ramón then stated that we should begin the meeting by deciding who should be the leader of the porra. I had not attended the previous day's meeting called to organize a collective strategy, but I imagined that this was part of the plan, even though it had not been part of Ramón's proposal the week before.

Ernesto quickly responded, taking back control of the meeting. He said, "I thought we'd discuss the more specific problems first and then come back to the larger problem of the porra's leadership at the end." Then he quickly changed the topic before anyone had a chance to respond.

Ernesto brought up the confrontation between porra members and the Neza fans that had occurred a week and a half before. Normally, when Ernesto brought up such an incident at a meeting, the porra members prepared themselves for a fatherly scolding. On this occasion, however, Ernesto took a different stand. According to the porra members I had spoken with, it was unclear who had initiated the confrontation against the Neza fans. However, Ernesto confidently stated that a group of close friends in the porra, including Gerardo, who call themselves La Rebel Plus, threw rocks at the bus and then ran away, leaving the rest of the porra to defend itself. Ernesto said that he had gone to his car and gotten his gun out of the trunk and stood ready to defend the porra. He held one porra member's actions up as an example of model behavior. Ernesto explained that this person had pulled his wife, sister, and daughter to a spot where they would be safe and then he had returned to fight. The idea being, I think, that this porra members' participation in the fighting showed the controlled and protective bravery of the paternal figure in contrast to the undirected violence of the desmadroso youth. As he described these actions, his voice rose with emotion.

When Ernesto finished his description, Juan, caught up in the excitement, described his participation in the fight as many porra members listened attentively or started to recount their own adventures of that day. With the future of his leadership in question, Ernesto had completed the twist he had begun to put on his usual argument about protecting women and children a couple of months before. He used his old metaphor of the porra as family, with its emotional pull, to justify physical violence, thereby also appealing to some of the young porra members' fascination with real or fictional fights. Furthermore, by focusing attention on what he strategically framed as La Rebel Plus's cowardly act, he diverted attention away from the question of his leadership and put some of his most vocal critics on the defensive.

Perhaps realizing what Ernesto was trying to do, Gerardo spoke up and asked, "Why should we pay for something a few fools started? Yes, I ran away, but why should I want to fight the [other team's fans]." For Gerardo, as for many of the young members, the solidarity of the porra and their physically rough behavior was meant to support the team, not to fight rival fans. No other members of La Rebel spoke, however, and Ernesto had already placed Gerardo in a defensive position. Gerardo seemed to lack his usual confidence. Ernesto simply ignored him and moved the meeting onto another topic. In a softer, fatherly tone Ernesto reprimanded Gerardo, asking him if they had not agreed that he and his friends would stop making banners with the name "Rebel" to hang in the stadium because the internal division was bad publicity for the porra. Gerardo, with his head hung in defeat, nodded in agreement without looking up.

The Creation of Confusion and Other Tactics

After addressing a few other issues that had nothing to do with his leadership, Ernesto held elections for two new positions, a vice-president and a secretary. He promised that these positions would spread out leadership among the porra members. Before the voting for the first position began, I asked Ernesto what the duties of the vice-president were because he had never specified them. Ernesto joked that the vice-president did not really have any duties, and everyone laughed. Then he said, "seriously now," and went on to give an answer that sounded to me like double-talk, although I wondered if my Spanish was in fact the problem. When I inquired about the duties of the secretary's position before the next vote, Ernesto just responded that the secretary was next in charge after the vice-president. In both of the elections, one of Ernesto's consentidos was defeated. Gerardo was elected to the position of secretary. After the meeting, Gerardo, José Luis, and Ramón recognized that the positions were a way for Ernesto to give his rule the legitimate appearance of democracy. They expressed hope for change in Gerardo's new position, although they were not sure how this might occur.

After the meeting, I asked Gerardo and José Luis if they had understood Ernesto's answer about the duties of the vice-president and secretary. They said they had not understood either. It seems to me that Ernesto did not want to specify the duties of these positions so that he could create the appearance of dividing up his power without actually having to do so. If the porra members did not know the specific duties of the positions, they could not demand that Ernesto give up those responsibilities. He avoided answering the questions by giving a response that was unclear, but close enough to making sense to confuse porra members as to whether they had missed something or whether they were being duped. Ernesto's tactic worked because porra members did not want to ask Ernesto to repeat what he had said and risk being ridiculed by their peers for having failed to understand. The next interaction that occurred at the meeting shows how such ridicule was used to deter most porra members from speaking up.

After the elections, Ramón suggested that they elect other members to occupy el poste because Juan, the current occupant of the position *no aguanta* (can't last) the whole game. Juan, with the aid of his charismatic personality and his domineering stance beside Ernesto, turned the suggestion into a pun by stating to Ramón, *No aguanto porque no me gustas* (I can't handle you [sexually] because you don't turn me on). Most of the porra members laughed at the double entendre, forgetting about the serious issue of el poste. Juan was able to divert attention away from the Ramón's criticism by appealing to the porra's self-portrayal as a group where humor and el desmadre, rather than seriousness and justice, hold legitimacy.

Ernesto, with his own stake in an image of seriousness and justice, finally quieted the laughter by saying that everyone should listen to Ramón. However, despite his display of support for justice and democracy, Ernesto responded to Ramón by talking about a completely different issue, once again using confusion to his advantage. He brought up the question of how the tickets to the games should be distributed, an issue that always absorbed the attention of porra members. After a brief discussion on the issue of ticket distribution, the meeting simply dissolved into groups of friends, discussing the weekend's parties and planning the next soccer season's adventures. No one brought up anything about electing a new cheerleader or a treasurer or about Ernesto's status as the porra's leader.

Later that day, I telephoned José Luis, hoping that he could explain why their attempts to bring about change at the meeting had failed so miserably. I wanted to know why there appeared to be almost complete consent to Ernesto's leadership during the meeting. I was curious as to why the dissenting members lacked solidarity, why they were silent about so many issues, and why they laughed at Ernesto's and his consentidos' jokes. José Luis answered that he was also confused about what had happened at the meeting and how everything could have ended up more or less the same. He did have a few theories about what had happened, however. José Luis repeated that most of the guys at the meeting were fairly new porra members, so that they do not understand the issues up for debate or Ernesto's tricks. Challenging José Luis's claim to experience and its superiority, I asked him why he, like all of the other members who claimed more experience, had not said a word during the meeting. He responded that he did not say anything because he was often confused about exactly what was being discussed. He said that even when he understood what was going on, he did not say anything because "you will just be ignored and laughed at when Ernesto's consentidos make fun of what you say." He seemed distressed by their inability to bring about change during the meeting, so I asked him why it appeared that most of the other porra members were not bothered at all. He said they were not troubled by what went on at the meeting because "they always do what they're told at home." I asked if he was different and if he could contradict his father. José Luis responded, "Yes, but not because I'm brave. That's just the way things are in my home." I do not know whether José Luis's attitude toward paternal authority actually differs from that of his fellow porra members. In fact, I imagine that many of them would make similar claims and none of them would admit to obedience, such behavior being characteristic of the despised América fans.

José Luis's statements could be read as saying that, although Ernesto's paternal act served to quiet some porra members at moments during the meeting, this cannot completely explain his success at silencing their dissent. I would add that his success depended, rather, on the use of a combination of what could be called micropolitical tactics including confusion and intimidation. Ernesto even turned the combination of these tactics into a tactic in itself. His rapid transformation of the contextual framework of the discussion, for example, from a familial to a democratic to a humorous context, contributed to the atmosphere of confusion he cultivated to silence dissent. While my main interest in this meeting is how it fits into a wider process of domination, struggle, awakening, and change that the porra was undergoing, much of what I have described was typical of all of the group's meetings and, I believe, typical of other examples of group organization in urban Mexico more generally. Most scholarly attention to Mexican leaders' co-optation of popular social movements and organizations has been directed to the creation of consent through patronage. The example of the porra's meeting, however, suggests that skilled leaders can create an appearance of legitimacy in a formal or state context, such as a meeting or an election, having established only a few key patron-client ties. As the interactions between Ernesto and the porra members demonstrate, a combination of subtle, micropolitical tactics can silence dissent for the duration of the meeting, creating what could be mistaken for a stable hierarchical social structure by an uninformed observer. Attention to this kind of strategy for silencing dissent may help to explain appearances of continued political stability in a postcorporatist era when national and local governments no longer have the resources to maintain a comprehensive network of stable patron-client relations.

The dissenting porra members' attempt to oust Ernesto from his leadership position was a resounding failure. The end of the meeting and the end of the soccer season also saw the end of their attempts to mold the Porra Plus into their ideal image. Their failure to bring about change, despite Ernesto's apparent willingness to listen to them and despite their strategic planning before the meeting, was a final lesson in a process of awakening that began when Javier left the group. First, under Ernesto's relative permissiveness, they became aware of their yearning to cheer in a manner that was incompatible with the hierarchical organization then dominant in the porra, with one cheerleader directing the rest of the group. Along with this discovery, however, they were confronted with the fact that Ernesto did not share this emerging vision of cheering and of the porra, nor did he even understand it. Even worse than Ernesto's misunderstanding of their wishes, they came up against the fact that Ernesto's democratic rhetoric was just a thin veil for his pursuit of personal interests with the team and with Nike. At this point, the porra members learned that such interests were not only problematic in an abstract sense, but in a practical one as well, because Ernesto's interests and supposed gains for the porra entangled it in restrictive relationships with patrons, which in turn interfered with the cheering style they were just starting to develop. Subsequently, when it became clear that Ernesto's interests, leadership style, and vision of the porra were at odds with their own, and the members attempted to resist his leadership or put an end to it completely, a new set of lessons had to be learned. Ernesto realized what the dissenting porra members were up to, and he put his tactics for deflecting dissent into

full gear, "spoiling" key porra members and discrediting others through a discourse of emasculation. Out of their growing
awareness of this situation of conflict and confrontation, porra
members developed defensive strategies and at the same time
a rebellious streak, epitomized by the emergence of a subgroup
calling itself La Rebel. Finally, in a series of struggles leading
up to and including the end-of-season meeting, the young porra
members learned an old urban Mexican lesson: if they continued trying to bring about change on Ernesto's terms, it would
only lead to the thinning of their ranks through co-optation (see
Vélez-Ibáñez 1983) and the humiliation of those who actively
resisted co-optation, such as Gerardo, or who were excluded
from it to begin with, such as Ramón.

In the next chapter, I extend this narrative beyond the period
of my initial field research, which ended soon after the meeting
described above, in May 1997. When I returned on a visit in the
spring of 1998, I was pleasantly surprised to find that the porra
members' desire for change had not been abandoned when they
discovered that it could not be achieved on Ernesto's terms. They
had founded a new porra and dubbed it "La Rebel." I will also
describe my findings from research conducted in 2004, when I
discovered a radically "Rebelized" cheering style among Pumas
fans and a Puma-ized style among fans of other Mexican teams.
Meanwhile, much of what the porra members had achieved in
1998 related to the group's internal organization had reverted
back to what most frustrated them under Ernesto.

6

Epilogue and Conclusions

La Rebel: The Emergence of a New Porra

The first section of this chapter is a continuation of chapter 5, in the sense that it continues to portray the porra as a process, through a narrative. I have decided to separate it, however, because what I describe here represents a new chapter or chapters in the porra's history and because I see the data upon which it is based as distinct. That is, what I present here is not based on the same kind of constant and intensive ethnographic research that led to the collection of the data presented up to this point. Rather, this narrative is based on sporadic visits to the stadium and occasional interviews with porra members concentrated in two periods, the spring and summer of 1998 and from May to December 2004. Therefore, I present general descriptions without much reference to the week-to-week interactions and individual actors. Despite the somewhat un-ethnographic character of these data, I believe they are worth including because they show even more clearly that what I observed during my period of intense fieldwork during 1996 and 1997 was not a simple snapshot of an unchanging reality but rather a social process in action. More specifically, in showing how this particular process continued and evolved, these data reveal the process as both cyclical or repetitive and as linear or historical.

As noted in the previous chapter, little changed in the porra following the meeting at the end of the spring 1997 season. What stood out most about the beginning of the fall 1997 season was not the tension between La Rebel and Ernesto but that Televisa had just purchased the rights to broadcast the Pumas' home games. As I stated in chapter 1, Televisa owns América and is closely associated with corruption, clientelism, and everything else that América stands for and the Pumas supposedly oppose, according to porra members. Not surprisingly, the porra members and many Pumas fans in general reacted with anger and some violence to this change. While they were disappointed with the team management's decision, they were also aware of the fact that it had to follow its financial interests and choose the best television offer available. Thus, most of the anger was directed at Televisa itself and its commentators there in the stadium, making it clear that they could buy the Pumas television contract, but not the fans. In an attempt to calm the porra and redirect its insults, Televisa invited Ernesto, as the group's representative, to appear on a radio show. Ernesto accepted and claimed during the interview that the porra had nothing against Televisa. When the porra members heard this, they redirected their anger once again toward Ernesto, stating that his claim on the radio reminded them that he was more interested in creating clientelistic relationships than with the group members and their principles.

1997 and 1998

Near the end of the fall 1997 season, the Rebel members started to plan the formation of a new porra, having given up on the possibility of ousting Ernesto and reforming the Porra Plus. Gerardo approached Ernesto and told him of the plan. Gerardo later recounted to me that he did so out of respect for Ernesto and avoided describing the move as a product of their conflicts. Ernesto wished him luck at the time, but then, according to Rebel members, starting spreading rumors that Gerardo was attempting to break up the group. Acting on these rumors, a couple of Ernesto's consentidos threatened Gerardo during one of the last games of 1997. At the start of the spring 1998 season, fifteen members of La Rebel established themselves in another section of the stadium, on the same side as the Plus but in one of the stand's corners, toward the southern end of the field. Gerardo purposely stayed away from the stadium the first couple of games to show the members of the Plus that the separation was not his personal decision, but rather the wish of the whole Rebel group. The Rebel members hung a banner in front of their section that simply said "Rebel" and implemented the kind of cheering they had been trying to bring to the Plus, standing, jumping, swaying from side to side, and singing the whole game. Rapidly their numbers grew, as porra members began to abandon the Plus and other young fans from around the stadium were drawn to the new group by its cheering style.

By the time I had a chance to attend a game and sit with La Rebel in March 1998, it already counted more members than the Plus ever had. The former Plus members were quite excited by this rapid growth and were also quick to note that much of it was at the expense of the Plus, which was, they said, shrinking. At one point during the game, their cheer was ¡*Somos un chingo y seremos más*! (We're many and we will be more!). They also boasted that they were much louder and desmadrosos than the Plus. When I looked over and observed the Plus, it appeared that it had shrunk a bit, but it was still substantial.

The Rebel's section of the stadium was marked off by two long blue and gold banners running the length of the section on both sides. However, the boundary was more porous than that of the Plus. They explained to me that anyone could enter the section as long as they cheered, and it seemed to me that there was no one on patrol as there always had been in the Plus. Beyond the new cheering style and this new more porous boundary, the Rebel members had implemented a couple of other measures in a conscious attempt to impede the emergence of the clientelism and other problems that had frustrated them about the Plus. First, while they had asked team management for permission to mark off a space in the stadium, they had not asked for anything else, such as free tickets, and had sworn to refuse any such offers. Second, the group was purposefully without a head.

This was apparent during the game because there was no one standing in front of the group to lead cheers.

The Rebel members explained to me that without a leader, it would be more difficult for the team management to gain control over the group through co-optation. Of course, without some sort of informal leadership, it would have been difficult to get cheers started. Gerardo and a couple of other original Rebel members were acting in this role. They were still also the main source of the group's growing repertoire of songs. Sometimes, I also noticed, one of this core of original members would turn to the rest of the section and implore everyone to cheer. These momentary acts of authority, meant to motivate cheering, did not seem to present a contradiction. In fact, at one point during the game, when the team was losing and the group had grown quiet, Juan, who had abandoned Ernesto for the Rebel's des-madre, turned around and shouted at those above him in the section, calling us *putos* (fags) and telling us to cheer. This com-mand reminded me of the days of the Plus and el poste, but when I asked José Luis what he thought of Juan's action, he said that it was good that Juan had tried to motivate people to cheer. Juan's attempt to command was forgiven because even more important for the Rebel members than these anti-authoritarian measures was the fact that we stood during the whole game and sang, tightly packed into a section so that swaying from side to side was not something I could have chosen not to do. When the Pumas scored a goal, the jumping up and down and piling on that occurred made the desmadre I remembered from the Porra Plus appear quite tame in comparison.

After the game, I accompanied my friends to the area of the parking lot where the players emerge from the locker rooms, where I encountered Ernesto. After a friendly chat, he asked me ¿Te *sentaste allá, no?* (You sat over there, didn't you?). When I responded that I had, he looked a bit hurt, but also resigned. Then we went over to where the Plus gathers before and after games and it seemed to me that there was no tension between members of the two groups, who were cotorreando as they always had. But when I encountered Samuel, the first thing he said was *¿Eres Plus o Rebel?* (Are you Plus or Rebel?). When I responded that I was just visiting, he appeared satisfied.

The next time I met up with Gerardo, Daniel, and José Luis, to watch the World Cup final at Daniel's house, I noticed that they spoke of the Plus with some bitterness. I asked if they hated Ernesto, and they responded in the negative, explaining that he was not a bad person, he simply had different objectives. Later, I heard stories of violent confrontations between the two group at games in other stadiums. According to Rebel members, these confrontations often started with the Rebel's verbal provocations followed by the Plus's violent defense, which never amounted to much due to the Rebel's superior numbers. Rather than leading these conflicts, however, Ernesto and Gerardo usually led attempts to calm the members of their respective groups.

2000 to 2004

I attended one game in the spring of 2000, by which time La Rebel had grown some but was still about the same size as in 1998. After that I did not attend another game until the fall of 2004, but I had the opportunity to observe games on television. By observing the occasional camera shots of the stands and listening to the singing in the background, I began to notice that the Pumas following had become "Rebelized" to a significant extent. That is, the type of cheering characterized by standing, swaying from side to side, and singing throughout the game was no longer confined to the Rebel's section. Rather, La Rebel was now initiating actions that many fans throughout the stadium were following. A stadium full of fans all standing and singing to support their team—a common phenomenon in European and South American leagues but not in Mexico—was precisely the goal that Rebel members had stated years before. What surprised me more about my observations via television, however, was that several other teams also boasted Rebel-like porras. Previously, teams such as América counted one or two porras with what appeared to be about fifty members, including adults of various ages and some women and children. Their cheering rarely went beyond an occasional Chíquiti Bom, the standard Mexican cheer adaptable to any team (see chapter 2). Watching games in 2003 and early 2004, I observed a number of *barras*, as cheering groups were now being called following Argentinean terminology, with 100 to 200 members standing, jumping up and down, and singing throughout most of the game. Furthermore, these groups now consisted almost exclusively of jóvenes, primarily men, but a good number of women as well.

When I talked to Rebel members later about these new groups, they admitted that these fans were sometimes acting on genuine emotion, whereas previously they took for granted that other teams' porras, especially América's, were on the payroll. This change could be described as the globalization of Mexican soccer supporters or more precisely its Argentinization, in reference to the most important foreign influence. However, on the national level, it could be seen at least partially as a Puma-ization or a Rebelization of Mexican soccer supporters, because, I believe, the other porras were copying not only what they observed on television from other countries, but La Rebel as well. It could be said that the young members of La Rebel acted as a conduit for a transnational flow of cheering styles to fans throughout the country.

In May 2004, the Pumas won their first championship since I had begun following them in 1996. I contacted Gerardo, Daniel, and Rafael, and we got together to celebrate at a *taquería* (a restaurant serving tacos) in my neighborhood. When they arrived they took off their jackets to reveal Pumas jerseys below. When I asked where they had seen the final, all three said they had gone to the stadium and that they would not have missed it for anything. I, ashamedly, had to admit that I had watched it at home on television. Gerardo and Rafael said they had paid 500 pesos for their scalped tickets, and Daniel had managed to get one through a player's family member.

This was the first time I had been around my informants after

Figure 6. La Rebel at the Pumas' stadium in 2003.
(Photograph by José Pedro Álvarez R.)

the Pumas had won a championship, and I found it interesting that what they seemed to savor most about the victory was that after a thirteen-year wait since the Pumas' last championship, they could finally get even with their workmates and classmates, fans of other teams, who had given them such a hard time over the years. Daniel, for example, described how he had cherished going to his office, where everyone despises the Pumas, after the championship and rubbing the victory in coworkers' faces. Rafael said that when he showed up at school after the victory with his jersey, and one of his classmates accused him of jumping on the Pumas' bandwagon. He returned the following day with a stack of more than ten years' worth of ticket stubs and exacted an apology from his classmate. This passionate evening of scores reminded me of the relational aspect of being a Pumas fan. Rather than relaxing among fellow fans, as is usually the case with single-team cities, my informants had spent their entire lives living among their rivals, and the significance of their fandom was as much a question of not being an Americanista, for example, as of being a Puma. Furthermore, these loyalties, in the case of Mexico City's fans, are not just to players, coaches, and team logos but to opposing manners of seeing and being in the world.

I was a bit surprised when Gerardo, Daniel, and Rafael all stated that this trip to the stadium for the final was a bit of a rarity for them these days. They explained that with commitments to work, graduate school, and girlfriends, their priorities were no longer the same. They stated that they would always be Pumas but they could no longer justify spending the time and money to go to games on a weekly basis. They added that going to the stadium was not the same for them as it had been during their last years with the Plus and the first years with La Rebel, because it is no longer a sure opportunity to spend time with close friends. Like them, most of the original Rebel members only rarely attend games and even when they do, the group is now so big that it is hard to find them. They mentioned a few who were now married, some with kids, and others who had simply disappeared. Rather than lamenting this change, Gerardo, Daniel, and Rafael seemed to find it quite natural and even expressed their disapproval of a couple of Rebel members who do continue to attend all of the games. They viewed these thirty-year-old hangers-on as somewhat pathetic because, instead of evolving in terms of personal and work relations, el desmadre was still the most important thing in their lives. They insisted, however, that their retirement from La Rebel was a happy one, because they had achieved what they had set out to do. They had left behind a stadium full of fans standing and singing throughout the entire game. Rafael recalled that the mentadas de madre in the Plus were fun at first but when they had gotten bored of this, they founded La Rebel. Now they had also become bored with that and had moved on to other things in other areas of their lives. Rafael's statement reflects the notion that Pumas fandom, like youthfulness, is representative of a broader social project applicable to life in general. Rafael, as well as Gerardo and Daniel, would always be Pumas fans but would now leave the ideal vision's flag bearing and defense to a new generation of jóvenes.

Gerardo, Daniel, and Rafael went on to tell me how La Rebel and its organization had also changed significantly. It had turned into a mafia whose leaders were earning enough to live on and live well. The team management, in its attempt to gain some control over the group, provided the leaders with a large batch of free tickets and with transportation to away games. The leaders, in turn, were selling the tickets and transportation to Rebel members as well as nonmembers and earning a considerable profit. In addition, they told me that the leaders had earned a considerable sum selling the rights to produce paraphernalia with the Rebel name, and they earned even more granting permissions to vendors to sell the paraphernalia in and near the group's section of the stadium. Gerardo compared what was going on in La Rebel to the manner in which the mafialike leaders of Mexico City's street vendors' organizations grow rich acting as intermediaries between vendors and government. Because of the Rebel's size and its members' impact as a potential violent threat, as consumers, and as triggers for others' consumption, this business had far surpassed anything that Ernesto had conducted in the Plus. Gerardo, Daniel, and Rafael recounted how Rebel members had threatened a coach and jumped on a sponsor's car to demand line-up changes. Regarding consumption, they mentioned the emergence of a significant market of official and pirated Rebel products, appealing not just to group members but to Pumas fans in general and even some young people uninterested in the team or the game. They noted that in the stadium one could observe as many people with Rebel t-shirts as Pumas jerseys.

I said that, although it surprised me that this shift back to clientelism and corruption had occurred so quickly, I had suspected the new porra would end up this way. Gerardo said that it was no surprise to them either. Although they had originally given La Rebel a structure specifically aimed at preventing this kind of regression, they always knew it could not last. He added that the main problem was that the group grew too large and it became impossible for them to maintain their influence, especially without the kind of hierarchical structure they specifically were trying to avoid. I inquired if they thought that all the Rebel members from top to bottom were equally corrupt and clientelized. When they responded in the negative, I asked if they thought there was potential for another revolution led by the uncorrupted and dissatisfied members. Gerardo responded that he had imagined such a thing might occur.

Thinking of the critiques of the increasing violence among Mexican fans, often attributed in the newspapers to the Argentinization of supporters and exemplified by La Rebel, I asked my friends if something of the sort was in fact occurring. Gerardo responded that there was no violence at all before, during, and after games because the police were doing a thorough job of keeping rival fans separated. They told me how the seating arrangement in the Pumas' home field had been completely altered for this very reason and also because of the increased attendance by Pumas fans. Previously, one whole side of the stadium had been reserved for visiting fans, even though only América, Las Chivas, and Cruz Azul drew enough to fill their half, whereas now visiting fans were allotted only one end of the stadium. Because the stands extend quite high up on the sides of the field but swoop down on the ends, this meant significantly fewer away fans at any game. This made confrontations less likely, but the police now also escorted the visiting fans into the stadium through a separate entrance and then escorted them out a couple of minutes before the games ended. Gerardo, Daniel, and Rafael also explained that when the Pumas play América in their home stadium, the police arranges for the Rebel members to meet at CU, to travel to América's home field with a police escort, and then to be escorted to their assigned seats in the stadium.

Gerardo, Daniel, and Rafael did, however, relate stories of violence. They said that one member of the current Rebel lead-

Figure 7. Heightened security at the stadium.
(Photograph by José Pedro Álvarez R.)

ership was staying away from América's stadium because the leaders of the latter's porra were blaming him for the death of one of their members and had threatened to take revenge. Daniel also recounted that when he was one of the Rebel's leaders a couple of years before, the police had stopped him in his car on the way into the Pumas' stadium and threatened to beat him if he did not stop attending games. Daniel somehow managed to escape the beating, but another one of the group's leaders at that time was not so fortunate. They speculated that the police had been sent by the team management in an effort to control the group by installing its own clients as leaders. In fact, Daniel did leave his leadership position after receiving the threats and now when he attends games he no longer sits with La Rebel.

Although these brief descriptions of a new sort of violence among fans hardly provides a complete picture of what is going on and why, it does seem clear that the confrontations are between rival porras or between team management and porra members and do not endanger other fans or the general public. In contrast, the media, often citing police and other government spokesmen, portray this violence as a general threat and claim that it prevents families from attending games, which in turn becomes a self-fulfilling prophecy as families are scared off by these reports. For example, an article in the February 9 edition of the sports daily El Récord reported that the *diputada* (the equivalent of a U.S. congressman) Rosalina Mazari, of the PRI, was proposing penalties of three months to two years in prison and fines between 30 and 150 daily minimum wages for persons involved in or inciting acts of violence in sports facilities (Redacción Récord 2005:15). Mazari was quoted as saying, "There is an increasingly marked presence of violent acts in stadiums and sports institutions, which create a real danger for those who attend in general; this is the case because there is no federal penal legislation regarding sports-related crimes" (Redacción Récord 2005:15, my translation). No proof was cited regarding the claim that there is a real danger for fans in general. The photographs that accompanied the article show a professional player striking another during a game and some young América fans climbing over a small wall in front of their section of the stands and approaching riot police protected by shields and helmets. While these photographs are hardly model images of peace, neither suggests any danger to fans "in general." My intention is not to justify the violence that does occur, but to suggest that its exaggeration and distortion by the media has further detrimental effects, such as unnecessarily keeping fans away from stadiums and encouraging potentially abusive police actions. Armstrong (1998) signaled a similar process in England where hooligans are portrayed and treated as a general threat and subjected to harsh legal penalties, when in fact their violent acts are directed at their rivals who are also their equals.

I attended the first game of the fall 2004 season with Gerardo. On the way into the stadium, we passed by the section of the parking lot where La Rebel gathers before games. I recognized and greeted a few people and Gerardo a few more, but in general most of the faces were new. When we bumped into Juan, we talked about the team's victory in the previous tournament. He seemed especially impressed by the atmosphere in the stadium, mentioning how when the game ended all the fans in the stadium were jumping up and down and even the players joined in on the field. Like Gerardo, Juan commented that they had achieved what they had set out to do with La Rebel. On the way to our seats, we were searched three times by security guards at three different points. In the days of the Plus, there was only one such checkpoint. After the body searches, we made our way to what previously had been the visitors' side of the stadium, but where La Rebel now occupies a large section at midfield. Gerardo asked if I wanted to sit right in the Rebel's section with the couple of old Plus members who continue to do so. He recommended, however, that we sit up a bit higher and just outside of the group's boundaries. He explained that he did not like having the Rebel's new leaders obligating him to cheer, because sometimes he just wants to watch the game. Gerardo also did not seem to like the idea of these younger Rebel members with a lot less experience than him and without knowing who he was or about his participation in the group ordering him to support the team. He said that one should sing when one feels like it and should not be forced. I noted that they had put similar demands on others when La Rebel first started, but he corrected me by saying that they had urged others to sing, but had not obliged them. Gerardo said that it particularly bothers him that the Rebel leaders sometimes try to obligate people sitting outside the group's section to cheer. I decided we should follow Gerardo's advice, and we sat level with the top of the Rebel's section, but about ten meters away, a good distance from which to observe the group and the other fans in front of us.

As the game was starting, Gerardo pointed out the number of fans in front of us—and thus not even in the Rebel's section—with Rebel t-shirts, and noted that he saw them for sale once at

El Chopo, a market known for its products related to rock and punk music. It seemed to me that there were almost as many as Pumas jerseys. The variety was also impressive: I noted about ten different designs just in the few rows in front of us. Common themes included Che Guevara's face and a skull-and-crossbones design with the Pumas logo (the cat's face) substituting for the skull. Gerardo commented that they put Che's face on the shirts without even knowing why, that they are simply copying Argentinean styles. I think the point he was making was that they don't even know what they are rebelling against, or in other words, they are not aware of the Rebel's history and what it was meant to avoid and to achieve. He said that they do the same things now with the songs, citing one case in which they adopted a song from Argentina without bothering to Mexicanize the specifically Argentinean lyrics. In contrast, Gerardo and the Rebel's other founders had always tried to appropriate rather than just copy the songs, making them meaningful for themselves as Mexicans and most of all as Pumas fans.

I also noted several banners hung along the top edge of the stadium, behind us and La Rebel. Some said "Rebel" and then the name of a neighborhood or section of the city, for example "Rebel Iztapalapa" or "Rebel Tlaltelolco." I noticed that most of the neighborhoods or sections of the city on the banners are associated with the working or popular classes, suggesting that the fan base is shifting and that subgroup affiliation based on neighborhood residence has emerged. There was also one banner that read "Auténtico Rebel" (Authentic Rebel). It is interesting to note that the ex-Plus and original Rebel members also seem to have become concerned with authenticity to an extent that they never were during my first period of fieldwork research (see below). Perhaps the growing number of fans and porras has led to greater competitiveness for legitimacy as true Pumas fans.

As we watched the Porra Plus cheer across the field from us, Gerardo commented that all they do now is copy La Rebel. He explained that, not only has the Plus adopted the Rebel's general cheering style, standing during the whole game and singing,

Figure 8. Banners expressing subgroup affiliations and fans
with the skull-and-crossbones insignia on their t-shirts.
(Photograph by José Pedro Álvarez R.)

but also that during games they are like an echo, repeating the
Rebel's songs and cheers just moments after. Gerardo said that
seeing this gives him a sense of satisfaction, because the leaders of the Plus had given La Rebel such a hard time about their
attempt to support the team precisely in the manner the Plus
was now using. It was apparent to me that his satisfaction was
not for the Plus, but rather in spite of it. The Rebel members had
been proven correct: their cheering style really was what most of
the fans were looking for, and the Plus's leaders had been self-
ish and foolish in their criticism and attacks. Straining to hear,
we also became aware of the continued existence of the Ultra,
the porra from which the Plus had broken off years ago. During
my time with the Plus, the much smaller Ultra had always been
regarded as the porra of the *burgueses y rucos* (bourgeois and
old men). Gerardo explained that it had maintained this repu-

tation, continuing the tradition of greeting the Pumas players and coach and of shouting witty comments and insults at the referees and opposing players, instead of singing. It had even drawn some of the older Plus members dissatisfied with its Rebelization. Gerardo also pointed out across the field a couple of other small porras that had formed recently. He said that one of them was founded by one of Ernesto's former consentidos from the Plus. He speculated that the former consentido must have wanted to start his own porra because he was close to Ernesto and saw all of his *transas* (tricks), but then realized that he would never receive a bigger share of the leadership or material benefits because Ernesto would not let go of what he had. He laughed about the diminutive size of these porras, including the Plus, in comparison with La Rebel.

After the game, we met up with a few other original Rebel members—who, like Gerardo, no longer sit with that group—and went back to one member's house. There, much of the conversation consisted of reminiscing about old times, including adventures in the porra and the Pumas' games and players. I was amazed, as I always was during such conversations, at their memory of the details of games played ten or fifteen years before. Beyond simple reminiscing, there was something competitive to the conversation as well, as they used the stories to demonstrate their knowledge of soccer in general and, in particular, of the Pumas' and the porra's history, thereby establishing their status as true fans.

The topic that most interested me, however, was their talk of how things had changed among the fans. For example, they stated several times that many of the current Rebel members go to the stadium more for La Rebel and its desmadre and not for the Pumas, and that many of the new Pumas fans in general cheer for the team because of its coach, the former star player Hugo Sánchez. At these points in the conversation, they would raise their voices and speak passionately, claiming that they are *Pumas de corazón* (Pumas at heart), first and foremost, and that if they participate in a porra, they do so to support the team.

At one point in the conversation, a couple of them claimed that they don't like to sit with La Rebel because you can't even watch the game with all the people telling you what to do and having to pass banners over your head that completely block your view. These critiques reminded me of something else I had observed during the game: in the middle of the Rebel's section a space cleared and Rebel members, bare to the waist, charged into the open space, jumping up and down and crashing into each other, in a scene reminiscent of a mosh pit at a rock concert. The participants, often with their backs to the field, could not have been observing much of the game. Then, someone brought up the proliferation of Rebel t-shirts as another example of their misdirected loyalties. I looked around the room and noted that everyone there was wearing a Pumas jersey, all of them expensive originals, although many were from past seasons. Rafael longingly noted that when you watch a European game on television all the fans are wearing the same color, which he said *se ve padre* (looks cool).

Another manner in which they phrased the authenticity of their fandom in relation to others was in terms of seniority. Rubén said that once an eighteen-year-old woman was shouting to fans passing by that she and her friends were the true Rebels. He quieted her by asking how that could be so if he had been cheering for the Pumas while she was still wearing diapers. Their donning of older Pumas jerseys was also no accident: it was a marker of the longevity of their fandom and thus of its authenticity.

Still another discourse for authenticating their dedication as fans, although employed by only a couple of those present, evoked willingness to fight and reminded me of the idiom of manliness and bravery that Ernesto used to discredit La Rebel (see chapter 5). Not surprisingly, the main proponent of this discourse was Rubén, from whom Ernesto had adopted this idiom at the time when Rubén and Juan were his principal consentidos. They recounted their participation in fights, emphasizing their individual bravery and that of a few others. They also compared themselves to other Pumas fans, without specifying who, but implying, I think, many of the Rebel's recent recruits, who talk and provoke but do not back up their words with actions or are willing to do so only when in a group.

I had heard porra members use such claims regarding passionate love for the team, seniority, and bravery to legitimate their actions and opinions before, with the Plus. But seven years later they sounded more passionate, perhaps because their lack of active membership in the team's currently most revered porra, La Rebel, left the authenticity of their love for the team open to some doubt.

While at some points during the conversation they were critical in this manner of newer fans, at others, they expressed their excitement over the team's rising popularity. They mentioned, for example, how after the Pumas' championship victory the previous season, the streets were filled with celebrating Pumas fans, honking their horns and waving flags out of the windows of their cars. They claimed that they had never seen a public celebration of that magnitude, at least there in the capital, for a championship team, including even the Pumas' previous victories and those of América and Cruz Azul. Gerardo fondly recalled the sense of camaraderie that was felt during a whole week after the championship as Pumas fans made themselves identifiable in public, wearing jerseys and hats and attaching flags to their car doors. He said that in those days as he greeted his fellow fans throughout the city, he gladly realized he was not so alone in his beliefs and convictions. Daniel added that another first was the fans' celebration at the Ángel de la Independencia, where previously fans had only celebrated the victories of the Mexican national team. He predicted that now that the Pumas fans had established this practice, that other teams' fans would do the same after their championship victories.

Rubén said that he had read of a survey that found that the Pumas is now the team with the largest following in the country, having surpassed even Las Chivas. I asked if they thought that this increase in the Pumas' following was due to their recent success or to the presence of Hugo Sánchez as coach. Rubén responded that, although he thought my reasons could account for some of the increase, they were not the main cause. Rather, he thought that it had something to do with los jóvenes getting interested in the team. I understood him to mean that more and more young people were seeing the world in the critical, passionate manner characteristic of Pumas fans. At that point he seemed like he wanted to say more, but was at a loss for words. The others present did not add anything either, although a few nodded their heads in agreement, leaving unanswered the question: why at this particular time are these young fans attracted to the Pumas and not to Las Chivas, América, Cruz Azul, or other teams? In the following section, I discuss why this might be and draw some other conclusions from this study.

Clientelism, Neoliberalism, and the Space in Between

This book has provided a look, through an ethnographic lens, at urban Mexico during a moment of significant political, economic, and social change. Since 1980, Mexico has seen the gradual weakening and dissolution of a half-century-old regime, spanning state and civil society, shaped like a pyramid, held together by clientelistic ties and fed by the economic growth of import substitution. This crumbling of the pyramid has been celebrated by some as the coming of democracy and lamented by others as the nightmare of neoliberalism in which individuals are cut free of all social moorings, leaving them exposed to the whims of global capitalism and in a state of identity-less disorder.

These two views, however, share a limitation: they are both developed from afar, often ignoring the realities of people's everyday lives. The first is blind to all but an emerging election-time democracy, neglecting the continuing presence of clientelism and coercion at multiple levels of society including, for example, professional soccer, as the porra members claim, and the porra itself, as I observed. The second view fails to resist

Figure 9. El desmadre in La Rebel, 2006.
(Photograph by José Pedro Álvarez R.)

adopting an old script in which unemployed, politically alienated young men, without proper leadership are imagined to
channel their frustration into rebellion without cause. In a manner similar to what David Harvey (1990) described among post-
modernists, the intellectuals and others who adopt this script
do so because they have confused their own and others' percep-
tions of disorder with social realities, when in fact these per-
ceptions are by-products of large-scale political and economic
change and destabilization. In contrast, a closer look at the
porra reveals both democratization and disorderly young men,
but much more as well, including a well-thought-out alternative to both clientelism and neoliberal democracy and a series
of contradictions and conflicts among these and other modes of
sociality.

Of course, the limitation of the closer look provided by the
ethnographic lens is its specificity. The porra members and my
observations hardly speak for urban Mexican society as a whole.

In fact, my decision to focus on a soccer cheering club may have seemed to some to be an especially esoteric choice. However, as I think this study demonstrates, soccer fandom, because of the game's publicly confrontational nature and its marginality, at least in Mexico, in relation to dominant nationalist projects, offers an ideal space for actors to congregate and to relatively freely imagine, contest, and implement different visions for the future. In other words, the goal of studying soccer fandom is not simply to fill a gap left by numerous studies of work, politics, and family, but also to capture the emergence of alternative social imaginaries. The narrative I developed in chapter 5 demonstrates such an emergence in reaction to Ernesto's rule, making it clear that what goes on in the stadium is not simply a symbolic expression of a supposedly "real life" outside, but rather involves creative, engaging, concrete action constitutive of the material world and instructive for understanding similar social processes in other contexts. Of course, the porra and even soccer fandom more generally exclude large portions of the population, but even such segregations are illustrative, suggesting how, for example, men exclude women and leaders marginalize certain clients in other urban social contexts.

The alternative social imaginary that I describe in detail here, with its focus on the expression of genuine heartfelt emotion, provides a previously unexplored subaltern critique of clientelism and neoliberal democracy and forces us beyond this dichotomy in our categorization of public socialities in urban Mexico. If urban Mexico is frequently imagined in terms of a struggle between its clientelistic, traditional past and its liberal, democratic, modern future, then the Pumas fans' ideal vision complicates this meta-narrative of modernization with another narrative containing an alternative possible future. As I suggested in chapter 2, this ideal vision complicates this meta-narrative at the same time that it is inextricable from both clientelism and liberal democracy, having, in a manner similar to Romanticism, emerged in reaction to clientelism and under the freedom provided by democratization.

The porra members' ideal vision obliges us to reject, or at least to rethink, other analytical categories as well. During a previous moment in urban Mexico, the categories of civil society and citizenship were difficult to apply. This is still true today, but the reasons have evolved. Before the problem was the ubiquity of patron-client relations, whereas now the porra members actively reject the likes of citizenship, with its externally imposed membership criteria, regulations, and rights. This point is most clearly illustrated in the disagreement between Ernesto and the young porra members over how to determine porra membership, described in chapter 2. While Ernesto tried to establish something like citizenship with objectively measurable criteria, the young porra members claimed that membership could only be determined by a fan's passion for the team, which, in turn, could only be felt and not measured. Along similar lines, the porra members' ideal vision also complicates the category of liberalism. Their ideal vision mirrors or perhaps even adopts aspects of liberalism, with its emphasis on self-government, in the sense that it looks inward for guidance. However, the members also reject the notion of free choice that usually accompanies self-government in this ideal liberal individual and consumer, instead stating that being a Pumas fan is something that one feels rather than chooses.

Youth is another example of an analytical category that the porra members compel us to rethink. They value their youthfulness, but as a means to a supposedly universal end, appropriate for those of all ages—the freedom to experience heartfelt emotion—and not as a fetishized end in itself, as in most youth cultures, nor as an intermediary age category, as in developmentally oriented studies.

The category class comes under scrutiny as well. The emergence of their ideal vision is tied to the frustration and freedom stemming from exclusion from economic opportunities and thus, I would add, to the notion of class. Yet group membership spans class boundaries in the form in which they are usually imagined in urban Mexico, showing how loyalty to their ideal vision overrides class loyalties, just as loyalty to clientelism does in other contexts.

A final example of how the porra members complicate frequently used analytical categories is that of masculinity. They make fun of typical representations of Mexican men through their performances of el desmadre, but their play involves the denigration of and aggression toward real women. As I noted in chapters 3 and 4, I have struggled to come to terms with the fact that their practices debunk and at the same time reproduce typical representations of Mexican masculinity.

I think that the porra members' uneasy relationship with these analytical categories, rather than proving these fans' exceptionality, instead suggests the limitations of the categories for understanding the complex social lives of a significant segment of urban Mexico's population, including, but not limited to, the porra members. Here, instead of conceptualizing urban Mexican society in terms of a battle of rich versus poor, young versus old, state versus civil society, or traditional versus modern, I have adopted local categories in the form of the ideal visions represented by the four national teams. In doing so, I have attempted to capture the dreams, projects, and divisions that constitute people's everyday lives in a manner that eliminates some of the distortion that comes with externally imposed analytical categories. As I have shown, it is not that such categories are irrelevant for understanding these soccer fans, but we need to pay attention to the manner in which actors adopt, question, and complicate these categories.

If porra members and others who share their ideal vision but not their taste for soccer constitute a significant segment of the population, they are far from dominant. As I showed in chapters 3, 4, and 5, the porra members see themselves and their social project as being under siege. The main threats parallel the dominant forces at the national level: a discourse of neoliberal democracy thinly veiling a weakened but still vibrant clientelism. Ernesto's discourse of democratization and his limited resources for creating and holding clients opened space for the porra members' refinement and implementation of their ideal vision. Still, they were not able to do so without having to face their president's continuous effort to suppress them, which in turn spurred them to create new strategies of resistance, such as their use of el desmadre as a protective mask and then their eventual total separation. However, this struggle continued even after their total separation, which resulted in the formation of La Rebel, when a brief victory against clientelism was followed by its forceful return in the new group.

This process shows that sociality in the stadium, and in many cases outside as well, can no longer be described as a set of stable clientelistic pyramids, although it is hardly a liberal paradise comprised of free-acting individuals either. Confrontation and conflict over the form that urban public sociality in contemporary Mexico takes are not only conceivable, they are inevitable. Now that no single mode of sociality is dominant, no agreement exists over the form the future should take, and many people are dissatisfied with the dominant options: a return to corporate clientelism or a continued shift to neoliberalism. Such conflicts and confrontations are not simply limited to the public sphere, however. As I argued in chapter 3, the young porra members' domestic and romantic interests accompany them into the stadium and, because of their siege mentality as Pumas fans, appear as a threat to their loyalties to the porra and their ideal vision. They attempt to disarm this threat, in a manner that parallels men's practices in other contexts, by blaming women for their own domestic and romantic leanings and excluding them from the group's core.

The persistence of this atmosphere of dissatisfaction, confrontation, and conflict into the first years of the millennium appears to be connected to the Pumas' rising attractiveness among young fans and to the Rebel's continued growth. As party politics fails to provide alternatives to corporate clientelism and neoliberalism—and in fact seems to be heading toward the extremes of these two poles if the contested 2006 presidential elections are any indication—dissatisfied, politically alienated, and often underemployed young people continue to find in the porra members' ideal vision a medium for expressing their frustration and an alternative way of achieving satisfaction. Further, the adoption of the name "Rebel" for the group and of symbols of rebellion and danger, such as Che Guevara and the skull-and-crossbones, seems to reflect the state of antagonism and conflict in which the fans feel themselves immersed. It is also important to think about the extent to which rising accounts of violence and heightened security at the stadium are due to the Argentinization of La Rebel and other teams' porras, as it often portrayed in the media, or to rising social tensions in contemporary Mexican society more generally.

It may be going too far to suggest that the porra members' ideal vision represents a potential alternative future for Mexican society as a whole, in the sense of completely replacing clientelism, neoliberalism, and other possibilities at the national level. In fact, their ideal vision seems precisely to evade the kind of systemization necessary to constitute a full social structure. However, rather than being a shortcoming, I think that this is precisely its point: that what Mexico needs are not more social systems, structures, or all-encompassing solutions, but a sort of antisystemic sociality that encourages and permits expression and enjoyment. The clarity of the porra members' proposal suggests that we are not talking here about a simple opiate meant to distract from life's inevitable exploitation and drudgery. Rather, I believe, we are facing a serious effort to deal with a pressing concern shared by innumerable people throughout the contemporary world, namely how to rouse ourselves from this modern nightmare in which we so often find ourselves living to work and govern instead of working and governing to live.

Notes

Chapter 1. Introduction

1. According to my more historically minded informants, "Goya" refers to the name of a café or, in some versions, a movie theater near the original campus of the UNAM in the city center where the male students took their girlfriends on dates. Some speculated that the cheer's apparently nonsensical lyrics (*cachún, cachún, ra, ra*) are derivatives of *cachundear* (to fool around sexually; to make out). While they could not explain how exactly this favorite hangout made its way into the team cheer, it is possible that the link is one of masculinity: the sexual conquest of girlfriends at the Goya being analogous to the defeat of rivals on the field. The university moved from the city center to its present location in the southern part of the city in 1954.

2. For further discussion and analysis of Chivas fans, see Fábregas Puig (2001).

3. Houses with both roofs and walls built of cement are often considered a sign of prosperity, in contrast to those built with tin roofs and adobe walls.

4. Ferry (2005) provided a thorough discussion of cooperatives in Mexico during this period.

5. See Armstrong (1998:13–20) for a fuller discussion of these hooligan studies.

6. Until the PRI's defeat in 2000, most of the recent Mexican presidents studied at the UNAM before earning a graduate degree in economics at an Ivy League school.

7. The stadium was the site of the 1968 summer Olympic games.

8. Both words, "Ultra" and "Plus," appear on the University's emblem.

9. See Nieto (2000) for further discussion of the class backgrounds and aspirations of residents of the four quarters of Mexico City.

Chapter 2. Being Puma

An earlier version of this chapter was published under the title "'You Can Buy a Player's Legs, But Not His Heart': A Critique of Clientelism and Modernity among Soccer Fans in Mexico City" in volume 9(1) of the *Journal of Latin American Anthropology*, copyright 2004 by the American Anthropological Association.

1. All translations from my informants' Spanish are my own.

2. Terms such as "modernity-as-means," "modernity-as-end," and "supra-ideological" are borrowed from Talmon (1967) and Grenier (2001a, 2001b).

3. Necaxa is a team with a small fan base that played its home games in Mexico City until 2003, when it moved to the city of Aguascalientes. Like América, the team is owned by Televisa.

4. While skin color and other physical features do not determine class status in Mexico, European features are undoubtedly associated with the elite and Indigenous features with the working class. In addition, beauty is often conceptualized in terms of Europeanness, and the looks of television and movie stars reflect this prejudice. Of course, such associations do affect class mobility even if they do not determine it.

5. At the end of each season, the first division team with the worst record over the past few seasons drops down into the second division and the champion of the second division ascends to the first.

6. In my interviews with porra members, they did not admit to any participation in clientelistic relationships at work. Furthermore, I was unable to observe them in their workplaces for more than brief periods, and therefore I was unable to discern their participation or lack thereof in clientelistic relations.

Chapter 3. A Day at the Stadium

1. At the time of the research, a short bus ride cost one peso and fifty centavos and a subway ticket cost one peso and thirty centavos. The exchange rate was approximately 7.5 pesos per U.S. dollar.

2. These young men living with their families have the freedom to go where they want and do what they want outside of their house, but for most of them, their homes are not places they can gather with their friends. Most of them do not have enough money to socialize in bars.

3. Games against América, Los Chivas, and Cruz Azul draw the most opposing fans, filling up the visitors' side of the stadium. The fact that almost all of the Chivas fans in the stadium come from Mexico City and

not from Guadalajara, the team's home city, demonstrates the national status of these teams.

4. One such chant was ¡*No queremos CONALEP*! (We don't want CONALEP!), which mockingly referred to a particular set of protests during the period of my fieldwork. Parents of students in secondary schools protested against a government decision to reduce the enrollment at public universities. A CONALEP is a technical school. Parents were protesting against having to send their children to technical schools in place of university.

5. In a big game, other porra members take up positions at the speaker poles in front of the adjacent sections to relay Juan's messages to the porra members and other fans sitting on either side of the group's main section.

6. I believe that the meaning of La Goya's words is not significant to the porra members, with the exception of the last word "universidad," referring to the National Autonomous University of Mexico (UNAM), which the Pumas team represents (see chapter 2 on the relationship between the university and the team). Rather, La Goya is meaningful to porra members because it is the cheer most directly and closely associated with the Pumas.

7. The reason for this focus seems to be less a question of xenophobia or prejudice than the fact that foreign players often stand out more because they receive more attention from the press.

8. I never heard the Mexican national anthem played before a league game at any stadium. It was, however, played before the national team's games.

9. Blue and gold are the Pumas' team colors.

10. I do not know to what extent an emphasis on creativity exists among fans in other countries. It is notable that when I asked porra members what was particularly Mexican about the porra, most of them referred to the creativity in the invention of witty comments and *albures* (sexual double entendres). In general, many Mexican men consider albures to be particularly Mexican. I would add that many Mexico City residents, but especially young men, practice a form of linguistic creativity in everyday verbal communication not limited to albures.

11. The diminutive of *consentidos* (favorite or spoiled children). See chapter 2 for a fuller explanation of the porra members' use of the term "consentido."

12. I refer to literary sources here because I perceive a gap or at least a weak spot in the anthropological and historical record of Mexican men's portrayals of or attitudes toward women and domesticity from outside the domestic sphere, that is, not as husbands, brothers, or fathers but as workers, anonymous men on the street, soccer fans, etcetera.

13. Vargas's use of "romanticism" to designate an historical period should not be confused with my use of the term to describe a social and literary movement organized around a particular set of ideas. She notes that the Mexican authors of the eighteenth century were, unlike their European counterparts, primarily concerned with unifying the country and nationalizing Mexican literature (Vargas 1994:83).

14. Gilmore (2001:224) saw the roots of such social tensions in a universal psychological dilemma in which men desire a regression to an infantile symbiosis with women at the same time that they must renounce their dependency on women to achieve full manhood. Although this argument has its appeal, evidence from the ethnographic record (e.g., Weiner 1976; Strathern 1988) questions the universality of the assumptions on which Gilmore's conclusion is based, that women are primary caregivers and that full manhood is tied to independence.

15. This preoccupation with divisions resonates with a position taken by the Unión Nacional de Mujeres Mexicanas during the 1968 student movement. This organization lamented the "gravely unstable and disruptive environment" and demanded that authorities "condemn the violence, defend our children" and effect a "return to normal life" (Carey 2005:58–59). Carey suggested that the women "used the rhetoric and vocabulary that the general public felt most comfortable with: that women in traditional feminine roles as mothers, sisters, and wives deplored the violence" (2005:59).

Chapter 4. Performing Motherlessness

1. Similarly, T. O. Beidelman (1980:35), as part of a critique of Victor Turner's universal notion of antistructure, suggested that, "Disorder and ambiguity serve different functions in different societies, and are manifest at different levels of the formal order of beliefs and behavior."

2. Historians Eric Hobsbawm and Terrence Ranger use the term "invented tradition" to refer to "'Traditions' which appear or claim to be old [but which] are often quite recent in origin and sometimes invented" (Hobsbawm 1983:1). Their oft-cited edited volume, *The Invention of Tradition*, pays close attention to the connection between such inventions and the "exercises in social engineering" necessary to the creation of nationalisms, nation-states, national symbols, and national histories (Hobsbawm 1983:13).

3. I refer here to how the porra members understand and experience such norms regarding the use of space, not to the original reasons for devising seating plans for this stadium or for modern stadiums in general.

4. When making pulque, the fermentation process may be initiated with a piece of human or animal excrement wrapped in a cloth. While this is not the only way to start it, this method has captured a large segment of the urban imagination. In addition, the thick gooey consistency of the drink is inconsistent with the tastes of many urbanites, who are more accustomed to drinks such as beer and brandy or tequila mixed with soft drinks.

5. Only in the last three decades have policies emphasizing centralization given away to efforts to decentralize the Mexican economic and political systems. Nevertheless, a continuing discourse of the need for decentralization suggests that the process is far from complete or successful.

6. While "reflexivity" recalls what some authors consider a particularly postmodern form of urban sophistication, the concept's similarity to the blasé attitude or ability to intellectually distance oneself from ones surroundings found in sociologist Georg Simmel's (1997:174–85) century-old description of urban life warns against exaggerating its newness (see Harvey 1990).

7. This "tradition" of celebrating important national soccer victories at this monument was begun just a few years earlier. Some informants suggested that the idea was invented and promoted by the Televisa network to increase interest in the national team, which it owned the rights to broadcast at the time.

8. This fear of a multitude of unconnected men in a public space is distinct from women's and men's worry about women finding themselves alone with an individual man or with a gang of men. I would venture to say that a preoccupation with the danger of an individual man or gangs of men is predominant in the United States, whereas the fear of a multitude of male strangers outweighs this preoccupation in urban Mexico.

9. Along these same lines, I suggest that the porra members are not in this case trying to establish or prove their masculinity, as suggested by Free and Hughson (2003:152) in their critical reading of some soccer ethnographies.

Chapter 5. The Porra as a Process of Domination, Struggle, and Innovation

1. Recent student movements protesting budget cuts and tuition increases at the UNAM are equally ironic. The protests uphold the university as the defender of the poor and egalitarianism, while ineffectively silencing the fact that it serves as a path for achieving or preserving class

status not available to all. Those who separate themselves from the protests make explicit the interestedness of those involved, even labeling them porros, and in so doing reinforce their status as authentically disinterested universitarios, a "disinterestedness" that serves to legitimate their continued participation in certain social settings.

2. I think that this is the result of historical change and not simply a different moment in the life-course of fans. During conversations with porra members in 2004, seven years after my initial fieldwork, I noted that in efforts to authenticate their fandom members did not mention their links to the university but rather long-standing love for the team (see chapter 6).

3. I call this authority "symbolic" because the bus drivers always seemed completely indifferent to all of the porra members' activities. I think that this symbolism nonetheless exists due to associations with school buses or even public buses over which the driver does have some authority. Ernesto completed the usual picture by sitting in the first row.

4. Héctor uttered this phrase in English.

5. Although not the standard porra profile, I never heard anyone criticize El Caco for these activities. Rather, he was respected for his fearlessness. At moments, however, his class distance from other members provoked some teasing, related, for example, to his pronunciation of certain words in a typical inner-city, popular manner.

Bibliography

Alabarces, Pablo. 2002. *Fútbol y patria: El fútbol y las narrativas de la nación en Argentina*. Buenos Aires: Prometeo Libros.

Archetti, Eduardo P. 1999. *Masculinities: Football, Polo and the Tango in Argentina*. Oxford, U.K.: Berg.

Archetti, Eduardo P., and Amílcar G. Romero. 1994. Death and Violence in Argentinian Football. In *Football, Violence and Social Identity*. R. Giulianotti, N. Bonney, and M. Hepworth, eds. Pp. 37–72. London: Routledge.

Armstrong, Gary. 1998. *Football Hooligans: Knowing the Score*. Oxford, U.K.: Berg.

Armstrong, Gary, and Richard Giulianotti, eds. 1997. *Entering the Field: New Perspectives on World Football*. Oxford, U.K.: Berg.

———. 2001. *Fear and Loathing in World Football*. Oxford, U.K.: Berg.

Bartra, Roger. 1987. *La jaula de la melancolía: Identidad y metamorfosis del mexicano*. Mexico City: Editorial Grijalbo.

———. 1998. El puente, la frontera y la jaula: Crisis cultural e identidad en la condición postmexicana. *Vuelta* 255:15–18.

Beidelman, T. O. 1980. The Moral Imagination of the Kaguru: Some Thoughts on Tricksters, Translation and Comparative Analysis. *American Ethnologist* 7(1): 27–42.

Bell, Catherine. 1992. *Ritual Theory, Ritual Practice*. New York: Oxford University Press.

Benería, Lourdes, and Martha Roldán. 1992. *Las encrucijadas de clase y género: Trabajo a domicilio, subcontratación y dinámica de la unidad doméstica en la ciudad de México*. Mexico City: El Colegio de México y Fondo de Cultura Económica.

Brandes, Stanley. 2002. *Staying Sober in Mexico City*. Austin: University of Texas Press.

Bromberger, Christian, Alain Hayot, and Jean-Marc Mariottini. 1993.

'Allez l'O.M., Forza Juve': The Passion for Football in Marseille and Turin. In *The Passion and the Fashion: Football Fandom in the New Europe*. S. Redhead, ed. Pp. 103–51. Aldershot, U.K.: Avebury.

Carey, Elaine. 2005. *Plaza of Sacrifices: Gender, Power and Terror in 1968 Mexico*. Albuquerque: University of New Mexico Press.

Chatterjee, Partha. 1986. *Nationalist Thought and the Colonial World: A Derivative Discourse?* Tokyo: Zen Books Ltd. for The United Nations University.

Cole, Jennifer. 2004. Fresh Contact in Tamatave, Madagascar: Sex, Money, and Intergenerational Transformation. *American Ethnologist* 31(4): 573–88.

Comaroff, Jean, and John Comaroff. 1999. Occult Economics and the Violence of Abstraction: Notes from the South African Postcolony. *American Ethnologist* 26(2): 279–303.

Davis, Diane. 1994. *Urban Leviathan: Mexico City in the Twentieth Century*. Philadelphia: Temple University Press.

Diouf, Mamadou. 1999. Urban Youth and Senegalese Politics: Dakar 1988–1994. In *Cities and Citizenship*. J. Holston, ed. Durham, N.C.: Duke University Press.

Dunning, Eric, J. Williams, and P. Murphy. 1987. *The Social Roots of Football Hooliganism*. London: Routledge.

Durham, Deborah. 2004. Disappearing Youth: Youth as a Social Shifter in Botswana. *American Ethnologist* 31(4): 589–605.

Edelman, Robert. 2002. A Small Way of Saying "No": Moscow Working Men, Spartak Soccer, and the Communist Party, 1900–1945. *American Historical Review* December:1441–74.

Elias, Norbert, and Eric Dunning. 1986. *Quest for Excitement: Sport and Leisure in the Civilising Process*. Oxford, U.K.: Basil Blackwell.

Escobar Latapí, Agustín, and Bryan R. Roberts. 1991. Urban Stratification, the Middle Classes, and Economic Change in Mexico. In *Social Responses to Mexico's Economic Crisis of the 1980s*. M. González de la Rocha and A. Escobar Latapí, eds. San Diego: Center for U.S.–Mexican Studies, University of California, San Diego.

Fábregas Puig, Andrés. 2001. *Lo sagrado del Rebaño: El futbol como integrador de identidades*. Zapopan, Jalisco: El Colegio de Jalisco.

Ferry, Elizabeth Emma. 2005. *Not Ours Alone: Patrimony, Value, and Collectivity in Contemporary Mexico*. New York: Columbia University Press.

Foucault, Michel. 1991. Governmentality. In *The Foucault Effect: Studies in Governmentality*. G. Burchell, C. Gordon, and P. Miller, eds. Pp. 87–104. London: Harvester Wheatsheaf.

Franco, Jean. 1989. *Plotting Women: Gender and Representation in Mexico*. New York: Columbia University Press.

Free, Marcus, and John Hughson. 2003. Settling Accounts with Hooligans. *Men and Masculinities* 6(2): 136–55.

Geertz, Clifford. 1973. *The Interpretation of Cultures*. New York: Basic Books.

Gilmore, David D. 2001. *Misogyny: The Male Malady*. Philadelphia: University of Pennsylvania Press.

Giulianotti, Richard, Norman Bonney, and Mike Hepworth, eds. 1994. *Football, Violence and Social Identity*. London: Routledge.

Goldstein, Daniel M. 2004. *The Spectacular City: Violence and Performance in Urban Bolivia*. Durham, N.C.: Duke University Press.

González de la Rocha, Mercedes. 1994. *The Resources of Poverty: Women and Survival in a Mexican City*. Oxford, U.K.: Blackwell.

Grenier, Yvon. 2001a. *From Art to Politics: Octavio Paz and the Pursuit of Freedom*. Boston: Rowman & Littlefield.

———. 2001b. The Romantic Liberalism of Octavio Paz. *Mexican Studies/ Estudios Mexicanos* 17(1): 171–91.

Gutmann, Matthew C. 1996. *The Meanings of Macho: Being a Man in Mexico City*. Berkeley: University of California Press.

———. 2002. *The Romance of Democracy: Compliant Defiance in Contemporary Mexico*. Berkeley: University of California Press.

Hall, Stuart, and Tony Jefferson, eds. 1976. *Resistance through Rituals: Youth Subcultures in Post-War Britain*. London: Harper Collins.

Handelman, Don. 1990. *Models and Mirrors: Towards an Anthropology of Public Events*. Cambridge, U.K.: Cambridge University Press.

Harvey, David. 1990. *The Condition of Postmodernity*. Cambridge, Mass.: Blackwell.

Hebdige, Dick. 1979. *Subculture: The Meaning of Style*. London: Methuen.

Hobsbawm, Eric. 1983. Introduction: Inventing Traditions. In *The Invention of Tradition*. E. Hobsbawm and T. Ranger, eds. Pp. 1–14. Cambridge, U.K.: Cambridge University Press.

Hobsbawm, Eric, and Terence Ranger, eds. 1983. *The Invention of Tradition*. Cambridge, U.K.: Cambridge University Press.

Holston, James, ed. 1999. *Cities and Citizenship*. Durham, N.C.: Duke University Press.

Lancaster, Roger. 1988. Subject Honor and Object Shame: The Construction of Male Homosexuality in Nicaragua. *Ethnology* 27(2): 111–26.

Limón, José E. 1994. *Dancing with the Devil: Society and Cultural Poetics in Mexican-American South Texas*. Madison: University of Wisconsin Press.

Lomnitz, Claudio. 1996. Fissures in Contemporary Mexican Nationalism. *Public Culture* 9:55–68. *See also* Lomnitz-Adler, Claudio.

Lomnitz, Larissa [Adler]. 1982. Horizontal and Vertical Relations and the

Social Structure of Urban Mexico. *Latin American Research Review* 17:51–74.

———. 2005. Los usos del miedo: Pandillas de porros en México. In *Jóvenes sin tregua: Culturas y políticas de la violencia*. F. Ferrándiz and C. Feixa, eds. Pp. 85–93. Barcelona: Anthropos.

Lomnitz, Larissa Adler. 1977. *Networks and Marginality: Life in a Mexican Shantytown*. New York: Academic Press.

Lomnitz-Adler, Claudio. 1992. *Exits from the Labyrinth: Culture and Ideology in the Mexican National Space*. Berkeley: University of California Press.

MacAloon, John J., ed. 1984. *Rite, Drama, Festival, Spectacle: Rehearsals Toward a Theory of Cultural Performance*. Philadelphia: Institute for the Study of Human Issues.

Magazine, Roger. 2000. Stateless Contexts: Street Children and Soccer Fans in Mexico City. Unpublished PhD diss., Johns Hopkins University, Baltimore, Md.

———. 2001. "The Colours Make Me Sick": America FC and Upward Mobility in Mexico. In *Fear and Loathing in World Football*. G. Armstrong and R. Giulianotti, eds. Pp. 187–98. Oxford, U.K.: Berg.

———. 2003a. An Innovative Combination of Neoliberalism and State Corporatism: The Case of a Locally-based NGO in Mexico City. *Annals of the American Academy of Political and Social Science* 590:243–56.

———. 2003b. Action, Personhood, and the Gift Economy among So-called Street Children in Mexico City. *Social Anthropology* 11(3): 303–18.

———. 2004a. Both Husbands and Banda (Gang) Members: Conceptualizing Marital Conflict and Instability among Young Rural Migrants in Mexico City. *Men and Masculinities* 7(2): 144–65.

———. 2004b. "You Can Buy a Player's Legs, But Not His Heart": A Critique of Clientelism and Modernity among Soccer Fans in Mexico City. *Journal of Latin American Anthropology* 9(1): 8–33.

———. 2004c. "¡Es puro desmadre!": El desorden y la violencia entre los jóvenes aficionados del futbol en México. *JOVENes: Revista de estudios sobre juventud* 8(21): 40–53.

Melhuus, Marit. 1998. Configuring Gender: Male and Female in Mexican Heterosexual Relations. *Ethnos* 63(3): 353–82.

Monsiváis, Carlos. 1987. *Entrada libre: Crónicas de la sociedad que se organiza*. Mexico City: Era.

———. 1995. *Los rituales del caos*. Mexico City: Procuradaría Federal del Consumidor-Era.

Nieto, Raúl. 2000. Multiculturalidad en la periferia urbana: La tensión entre lo público y lo privado. *Nueva Antropología* 17(57): 57–67.

O'Malley, Ilene V. 1986. *The Myth of Revolution: Hero Cults and the*

Institutionalization of the Mexican State, 1920–1940. New York: Greenwood Press.

Paley, Julia. 2001. *Marketing Democracy*. Berkeley: University of California Press.

Pansters, Wil G. 1997. Theorizing Political Culture in Modern Mexico. In *Citizens of the Pyramid: Essays on Mexican Political Culture*. W. Pansters, ed. Amsterdam: Thela.

Paz, Octavio. 1961. *The Labyrinth of Solitude: Life and Thought in Mexico*. New York: Grove Press.

Poniatowska, Elena. 1971. *La noche de Tlaltelolco: testimonios de historia oral*. Mexico City: Era.

Prieur, Annick. 1998. *Mema's House, Mexico City: On Transvestites, Queens, and Machos*. Chicago: University of Chicago Press.

Redacción Récord. 2005. ¿Fin al problema?: El gobierno quiere erradicar la violencia. In *El Récord*. 9 February, p. 15. México, D.F.

Redhead, Steve, ed. 1993. *The Passion and the Fashion: Football Fandom in the New Europe*. Aldershot, U.K.: Avebury.

Robson, Garry. 2000. *"No One Likes Us, We Don't Care": The Myth and Reality of Millwall Fandom*. Oxford, U.K.: Berg.

Rodríguez Aguilar, Edgar. 2005. *Vuelta al laberinto de la modernidad: Análisis de momentos clave del diálogo en el movimiento estudiantil de 1999*. Mexico City: Instituto Mexicano de la Juventud.

Roniger, Luis. 1990. *Hierarchy and Trust in Modern Mexico and Brazil*. New York: Praeger.

Rubenstein, Anne. 2001. Bodies, Cities, Cinema: Pedro Infante's Death as Political Spectacle. In *Fragments of a Golden Age: The Politics of Culture in Mexico since 1940*. G. Joseph, A. Rubenstein, and E. Zolov, eds. Pp. 199–233. Durham, N.C.: Duke University Press.

Simmel, Georg. 1997. *Simmel on Culture: Selected Writings*. London: Sage.

Strathern, Marilyn. 1988. *The Gender of the Gift: Problems with Women and Problems with Society in Melanesia*. Berkeley: University of California Press.

Talmon, J. L. 1967. *Romanticism and Revolt: Europe 1815–1848*. London: Thames and Hudson.

Turner, Victor. 1969. *The Ritual Process*. Chicago: Aldine.

——. 1982. *Celebration: Studies in Festivity and Ritual*. Washington, D.C.: Smithsonian Institution Press.

Urteaga Castro-Pozo, Maritza. 1998. *Por los territorios del rock: Identidades juveniles y rock Mexicano*. Mexico City: Causa Joven y Consejo Nacional para la Cultura y las Artes.

Vargas, Margarita. 1994. Romanticism. In *Mexican Literature: A History*. D. W. Foster, ed. Pp. 83–112. Austin: University of Texas Press.

Vélez-Ibáñez, Carlos G. 1983. *Rituals of Marginality: Politics, Process, and Culture Change in Urban Central Mexico, 1969–1974*. Berkeley: University of California Press.

Verkaaik, Oscar. 2004. *Migrants and Militants: Fun and Urban Violence in Pakistan*. Princeton, N.J.: Princeton University Press.

Weiner, Annette B. 1976. *Women of Value, Men of Renown: New Perspectives on Trobriand Exchange*. Austin: University of Texas Press.

Zermeño, Sergio. 1996. *La sociedad derrotada: El desorden mexicano del fin de siglo*. Mexico City: Siglo Veintiuno.

Zolov, Eric. 1999. *Refried Elvis: The Rise of the Mexican Counterculture*. Berkeley: University of California Press.

Index

About the Author

Roger Magazine is a research professor in the Graduate Program in Social Anthropology in the Department of Social and Political Sciences of the Universidad Iberoamericana in Mexico City. He received his PhD in anthropology from The Johns Hopkins University. He is the author of several articles and book chapters on soccer fans and street youth in Mexico City. Currently, he is conducting research on the effects of and reactions to urban expansion in a village outside the Mexican capital.